BANKING AND BANKING DEVELOPMENTS

COMMERCIAL REAL ESTATE LENDING

RISK MITIGATION AND BANK SUPERVISION

BANKING AND BANKING DEVELOPMENTS

Additional books in this series can be found on Nova's website under the Series tab.

Additional E-books in this series can be found on Nova's website under the E-book tab.

FINANCIAL INSTITUTIONS AND SERVICES

Additional books in this series can be found on Nova's website under the Series tab.

Additional E-books in this series can be found on Nova's website under the E-book tab.

BANKING AND BANKING DEVELOPMENTS

COMMERCIAL REAL ESTATE LENDING

RISK MITIGATION AND BANK SUPERVISION

OLIVER R. SIMS
AND
FRANKLIN B. FIELDS
EDITORS

nova publishers
New York

For permission to use material from this book please contact us:
Telephone 631-231-7269; Fax 631-231-8175
Web Site: http://www.novapublishers.com

Library of Congress Cataloging-in-Publication Data

ISBN: 978-1-62618-617-0

Published by Nova Science Publishers, Inc. † New York

CONTENTS

Preface

This book presents the results of a study of FDIC-supervised institutions with significant acquisition, development, and construction (ADC) loan concentrations that did not fail during the recent economic downturn. ADC loans are considered the riskiest type of commercial real estate (CRE) lending. During the recent financial crisis, FDIC analysis shows that failed institutions had concentrations of ADC loans to total assets that were roughly three times the average of concentrations of non-failed institutions. This book studies the characteristics and supervisory approaches for FDIC-supervised institutions that had significant ADC loan concentrations in December 2007 and were not considered to be problem banks as of April 2011, with a focus on the identifying factors that may have helped banks mitigate the risks historically associated with ADC concentrations during periods of economic stress.

Chapter 1 - This report presents the results of our study of FDIC-supervised institutions with significant acquisition, development, and construction (ADC) loan concentrations that did not fail during the recent economic downturn. ADC loans are considered the riskiest type of commercial real estate (CRE) lending. During the recent financial crisis, FDIC analysis shows that failed institutions had concentrations of ADC loans to total assets that were roughly three times the average of concentrations of non-failed institutions.

Our objective was to study the characteristics and supervisory approaches for FDIC-supervised institutions that had significant ADC loan concentrations in December 2007 and were not considered to be problem banks as of April 2011. In initiating this study, we were interested in identifying factors that may have helped banks mitigate the risks historically associated with ADC concentrations during periods of economic stress.

To evaluate the characteristics of the banks included in our study, we reviewed key financial ratios for the FDIC-supervised institutions meeting the criteria of our study – generally in satisfactory condition and having concentrations that regulators considered to be significant – and the 214 FDIC-supervised institutions that failed between January 2007 and April 2011. Doing so allowed us to compare and contrast the two groups. We also contacted bank officials for a sample of the institutions and discussed their strategies for managing ADC concentrations and factors, which in their view, allowed their institutions to remain fundamentally sound or to successfully overcome the risk and losses associated with the concentrations. To evaluate the FDIC's supervisory approach, we reviewed the supervisory documents, including any enforcement actions taken, for a sample of banks that we refer to as "turn- around" banks. That is, banks with significant ADC concentrations in December 2007, some level of supervisory concern between 2007 and 2010, and improved supervisory ratings as of April 2011.

Chapter 2 - Since the onset of the financial crisis in 2008, commercial real estate (CRE) loan delinquencies have more than doubled. The federal banking regulators have issued statements and guidance encouraging banks to continue lending to creditworthy borrowers and explaining how banks can work with troubled borrowers. However, some banks have stated that examiners' treatment of CRE loans has hampered their ability to lend. This report examines, among other issues, (1) how the Federal Deposit Insurance Corporation (FDIC), Board of Governors of the Federal Reserve System (Federal Reserve), and the Office of the Comptroller of the Currency (OCC) responded to trends in CRE markets and the controls they have for helping ensure consistent application of guidance and (2) the relationships between bank supervision practices and lending. GAO reviewed agency guidance, examination review procedures, reports of examination, and relevant literature and interviewed agency officials, examiners, bank officials, and academics.

In: Commercial Real Estate Lending
Editors: O. R. Sims and F. B. Fields
ISBN: 978-1-62618-617-0

Chapter 1

ACQUISITION, DEVELOPMENT, AND CONSTRUCTION LOAN CONCENTRATION STUDY*

Federal Deposit Insurance Corporation

EXECUTIVE SUMMARY

Why We Did the Evaluation

This report presents the results of our study of FDIC-supervised institutions with significant acquisition, development, and construction (ADC) loan concentrations that did not fail during the recent economic downturn. ADC loans are considered the riskiest type of commercial real estate (CRE) lending. During the recent financial crisis, FDIC analysis shows that failed institutions had concentrations of ADC loans to total assets that were roughly three times the average of concentrations of non-failed institutions.

Our objective was to study the characteristics and supervisory approaches for FDIC-supervised institutions that had significant ADC loan concentrations in December 2007 and were not considered to be problem banks as of April 2011. In initiating this study, we were interested in identifying factors that may

---

* This is an edited, reformatted and augmented version of the Office of Audits and Evaluations, Report No. EVAL-13-001, dated October 2012.

have helped banks mitigate the risks historically associated with ADC concentrations during periods of economic stress.

To evaluate the characteristics of the banks included in our study, we reviewed key financial ratios for the FDIC-supervised institutions meeting the criteria of our study – generally in satisfactory condition and having concentrations that regulators considered to be significant – and the 214 FDIC-supervised institutions that failed between January 2007 and April 2011. Doing so allowed us to compare and contrast the two groups. We also contacted bank officials for a sample of the institutions and discussed their strategies for managing ADC concentrations and factors, which in their view, allowed their institutions to remain fundamentally sound or to successfully overcome the risk and losses associated with the concentrations. To evaluate the FDIC's supervisory approach, we reviewed the supervisory documents, including any enforcement actions taken, for a sample of banks that we refer to as "turn- around" banks. That is, banks with significant ADC concentrations in December 2007, some level of supervisory concern between 2007 and 2010, and improved supervisory ratings as of April 2011.

Background

History has demonstrated that CRE markets can experience fairly rapid changes. Specifically, according to the FDIC's *History of the Eighties–Lessons for the Future*, investment in CRE has traditionally been quite risky. Real estate markets as a whole are traditionally cyclical, so that even the most well-conceived and soundly underwritten CRE project can become troubled during the periodic overbuilding cycles that characterize these markets. ADC lending is generally considered to be the riskiest class of CRE due to long development times and because ADC lending can include properties that are built before having firm commitments from buyers or lessees. In addition, by the time the construction phase is completed, market demand may have fallen – placing downward pressure on sales prices or rents – making this type of loan more volatile.

Between 2001 and 2008, ADC lending grew rapidly at FDIC-insured banks. To address the growth in CRE concentrations, the banking regulatory agencies issued joint guidance in December 2006, which was intended to reinforce existing regulations and guidelines for real estate lending and safety and soundness. However, by the summer of 2007, a series of complex and interrelated shocks began to unfold, sparking sharp declines in real estate values in many regions of the country and setting off a wave of bank failures beginning in 2008.

Evaluation Results

We identified 436 institutions that met our criteria of having an ADC concentration of 100 percent or greater as of December 2007 and were in satisfactory condition as of April 2011. We focused attention on a sample of 18 of those institutions that had ADC concentrations of 300 percent or more. We took this approach because, in our view, the experience of these 18 institutions was unique and allowed us to readily compare their practices to those institutions with ADC concentrations that failed. Notably, we did not identify a significant number of banks with high concentrations in 2007 that were in satisfactory condition in 2011.

We believe this is reflective of how difficult it is for institutions with exceedingly high ADC concentrations to mitigate the concentration risk during an economic downturn. Perhaps not surprisingly, bankers we interviewed characterized the Board's and management's risk appetite to be conservative or moderate. These same bankers implemented many of the key elements of the risk management framework that regulators have said are needed to manage ADC concentrations. Additionally, bankers we spoke to indicated that they limited speculative lending, loan participations, and out-of-area lending. Finally, a number of bankers were quick to point out that their market areas were less impacted by the economic decline.

As a result of these factors, banks in our study did not experience significant losses from their ADC portfolio and managed to maintain stable capital positions even with a steep and prolonged economic decline.

We found that the supervisory approach and level of supervisory attention for the 23 turn-around banks we sampled were generally consistent with the FDIC's supervisory practices and policies and similar to the approach for banks that ultimately failed. That is, as economic conditions declined and banks' financial condition began to weaken, the FDIC's supervisory attention increased and supervisory actions were pursued. However, we observed that the approach yielded a better outcome – stable or improved examination ratings – because turn-around banks were responsive to supervisory actions and guidance and maintained or secured capital needed to absorb losses in response to regulatory demands.

Observations and Matters for Consideration

Prior to the recent financial crisis, competition among financial institutions for growth, profitability, and community influence often resulted in the compromise of sound credit principles and acquisition of unsound loans. Ultimately, that type of compromise resulted in a spate of bank failures not seen since the 1980s—a period that, in broad terms, was not that long ago. Much was written following the banking crisis of the 1980s and early 1990s, and there were ample discussions of lessons learned.

In addition, far- reaching legislative and regulatory actions were taken and extensive guidance was issued by regulators on key risks, including repeated warnings and references to best practices related to ADC lending because it is a highly specialized field with inherent risks that must be managed and controlled. Nevertheless, unlike the circumstances at the banks we studied, Boards and management at too many other institutions pursued profits through growth and higher-earning, risky assets, in an era of easy credit, while lacking robust risk management practices—a story that appears very similar to the one told just over 20 years ago.

We found that some institutions with ADC concentrations were able to weather the recent financial crisis without experiencing a corresponding decline in their overall financial condition. The factors that contributed to their survival validate the point that regulators have emphasized and reiterated for years – a well-informed and active Board, strong management, sound credit administration and underwriting practices, and adequate capital are important in managing ADC concentrations in a safe and sound manner. In addition, the banks in our study did not rely on brokered deposits to fund growth, and geographic location factored into the degree of ADC loan losses. Ultimately, the strategic decisions and disciplined, values-based practices and actions taken by the Boards and management helped to mitigate and control the institutions' overall ADC loan risk exposure and allowed them to react to a changing economic environment. Unlike many failed banks that saw their capital evaporate rapidly because of the losses associated with their ADC portfolios, the banks in our study experienced comparatively fewer losses and were able to maintain stable capital positions.

Further, we determined that the FDIC's supervisory approach and level of supervisory attention for the turn-around banks were generally consistent with the FDIC's supervisory practices and policies and similar to the approach for failed banks. In that regard, the following areas in which the FDIC has implemented revised supervisory policies and procedures are worth highlighting.

- While the supervisory approach we observed for turn-around banks proved effective, similar to observations made in our material loss reviews (MLRs), we believe that earlier emphasis on risk management practices would have been beneficial. To that end, the Corporation completed a training initiative in 2010 for its entire supervisory workforce that focused on placing greater emphasis on risk management practices for institutions with elevated risk profiles. The training addressed the importance of considering management practices as well as current financial performance or trends when assigning ratings, consistent with existing examination guidance. This approach encourages bank management to continuously implement effective risk management practices and examiners to promptly address control weaknesses, regardless of how well a bank is performing financially.
- Management's responsiveness to supervisory concerns was a key differentiating factor between banks that failed and the turn-around banks we reviewed. Generally, our MLRs have shown that examiners identified significant risks but did not take timely and effective action to address those risks until the bank had started to experience significant financial deterioration in the loan or investment portfolios. In response to those findings, the FDIC has conducted training and issued guidance aimed at timely communication of risks to financial institutions, prompt supervisory and enforcement actions, and examiner follow-up. The Corporation should remain vigilant in ensuring that its processes and examiners sufficiently promote prompt and effective responses to examination findings and supervisory actions, including timely and progressive enforcement of situations involving banks that are not responsive to examination findings, repeat criticisms, or violations.

Finally, the FDIC has to date, and must continue to make certain, that lessons learned associated with ADC concentrations become ingrained in day-to-day supervisory activities and that placing greater emphasis on risk management practices for institutions with elevated risk profiles is sustained regardless of the health of the economy or banking industry or the political appetite for financial regulation. We trust that the analysis and conclusions of our study will benefit the Corporation and assist in management's continuous efforts to have an efficient and effective supervisory program that protects depositors and the Deposit Insurance Fund.

Corporation Comments

We provided a draft of this report to FDIC management on August 9, 2012. The FDIC was not required to provide a written response because the report contained no recommendations, and management opted to only provide informal comments regarding the technical accuracy of certain report content. We made changes to the report, where appropriate, to address those comments. FDIC management did express general agreement with the evaluation results at the exit conference for this assignment.

DATE:	October 31, 2012
MEMORANDUM TO:	Sandra L. Thompson, Director Division of Risk Management Supervision
	/Signed/
FROM:	Stephen M. Beard Deputy Inspector General for Audits and Evaluations
SUBJECT:	*Acquisition, Development, and Construction Loan Concentration Study* (Report No. EVAL-13-001)

This report presents the results of our study of FDIC-supervised institutions[1] with significant *acquisition, development, and construction*[2] loan (ADC) *concentrations* that did not fail during the recent economic downturn. ADC loans are considered the riskiest type of *commercial real estate* (CRE) lending. During the recent financial crisis, FDIC analysis shows that failed institutions had concentrations of ADC loans to total assets that were roughly three times the average of concentrations of non-failed institutions.

In presenting these results, we are mindful that FDIC-supervised institutions and the FDIC itself have already learned key lessons associated with ADC loan concentrations. Banks are modifying borrowers' loan terms so that they can continue to make payments; increasing bank capital and reserves as protection against future losses; and, in some cases, reducing lending. The

FDIC and the other federal banking regulators have responded by issuing interagency statements and guidance on managing the risks of ADC concentrations, encouraging banks to continue lending to creditworthy borrowers, clarifying to banks how examiners will review loans secured by real estate, and explaining how banks can work with troubled borrowers. While there has been some improvement in the market, problems in this type of lending are expected to continue and could present further challenges to the market in coming years.

With that in mind, it was our intention in this report to shift the focus away from banks that failed to those that managed to see their way through the economic downturn and maintain safe and sound operations. Likewise, the intent of the study was to focus on the FDIC's supervisory approach to ADC concentrations in banks that remained open rather than evaluate what examiners did to minimize loss to the Deposit Insurance Fund (DIF) as a result of an institution that had failed. To provide a context for our results, the report first presents background information addressing the extent to which FDIC-insured banks grew their ADC loan portfolios during the financial crisis and how that growth contributed to failures and then summarizes key supervisory guidance and tenets of sound risk management associated with ADC concentrations. The next two sections of our report discuss (1) the common characteristics of the banks we studied and how they contrast with those that failed and (2) how the supervisory approach and level of supervisory attention for the banks we sampled compared to those banks that ultimately failed. Finally, we provide our concluding observations and matters for management's consideration.

EVALUATION OBJECTIVE AND APPROACH

Our objective was to study the characteristics and supervisory approaches for FDIC-supervised institutions that had significant ADC loan concentrations in December 2007 and were not considered to be problem banks as of April 2011. In initiating this study, we were interested in identifying factors that may have helped banks mitigate the risks historically associated with ADC concentrations during periods of economic stress.

We identified 436 institutions meeting our criteria – that is, institutions with ADC concentrations 100 percent or greater as of December 2007 and considered to be in a satisfactory condition as of April 2011.[3] We used 100 percent as a benchmark because it is the threshold that regulators use to identify institutions that are potentially exposed to significant CRE concentration risk, which is described in guidance entitled, *Concentrations in Commercial Real Estate Lending, Sound Risk Management Practices* (Joint Guidance).[4]

To study the characteristics of these banks, we performed level and trend analysis of key financial ratios for the 436 FDIC-supervised institutions we identified and the 214 FDIC-supervised institutions that failed between January 2007 and April 2011.[5] Doing so allowed us to compare and contrast the two groups. Of the 436 institutions, we focused attention on a sample of 18 institutions that had concentrations of 300 percent or greater and were in satisfactory condition to determine whether these institutions had any unique characteristics that we could learn from. We also reviewed an FDIC-generated loan underwriting survey to understand the risk profile of sound banks with ADC concentrations, which we compared with the FDIC-supervised banks that failed.

To study the FDIC's supervisory approach, we looked at banks with ADC concentrations between 100 and 300 percent as of December 2007 that were in a less-than-satisfactory condition between 2007 and 2010 and subsequently received a higher composite rating as of April 2011. We identified 71 institutions meeting these criteria and selected a non-statistical sample of 23 banks, which we refer to as "turn-around" banks in this report. [6] For each of the 23 turn-around banks, we obtained and reviewed key supervisory documents for our scope period, January 2007 through June 2011.

Lastly, we contacted bank officials in 38 institutions to discuss their strategies for managing ADC concentrations and factors, which in the officials' view, allowed their institutions to remain fundamentally sound or to successfully overcome the risk and losses associated with the concentrations. We also solicited their views on the FDIC's supervision with respect to ADC concentrations. Among the banks we contacted were officials from (1) all 18 banks in our sample of institutions that had concentrations of 300 percent or greater and were in satisfactory condition and (2) about half of our sample of turn-around banks. Thirty-six bank officials agreed to talk with us. The results of our discussions are reflected throughout the report. However, to avoid overstating the precision of the results, we use the terms "few," "some," and "most."[7] We did not interview officials in banks with high ADC concentrations that were considered to be in a less-than-satisfactory condition as of April 2011 because those banks were not a focus of this study. Therefore, the experiences and views of those officials may differ from those of the officials we interviewed and are not reflected in this report except where we reference results from a Government Accountability Office (GAO) study on CRE.

Our basic understanding of the risks associated with ADC concentrations is based on our review of regulatory guidance and ADC-related reports, including reports from GAO and the FDIC. We also considered *material loss* review (MLR) reports[8] issued by our office and other studies written about bank failures during the recent financial crisis to identify issues associated with ADC concentrations discussed in those reports.

We performed our evaluation work from July 2011 through February 2012 in accordance with the Council of the Inspectors General on Integrity and Efficiency's *Quality Standards for Inspection and Evaluation*. Appendix 1 includes additional details related to our objective, scope, and methodology. Appendix 2 provides a glossary of certain terms used in this report, and Appendix 3 provides a list of acronyms also used in this report.

BACKGROUND

According to the FDIC's *History of the Eighties–Lessons for the Future*, investment in CRE has traditionally been quite risky. Real estate markets as a whole are traditionally cyclical, so that even the most well-conceived and soundly underwritten CRE project can become troubled during the periodic overbuilding cycles that characterize these markets. ADC lending is generally considered to be the riskiest class of CRE due to long development times and because ADC lending can include properties that are built before having firm commitments from buyers or lessees. In addition, by the time the construction phase is completed, market demand may have fallen – placing downward pressure on sales prices or rents – making this type of loan more volatile. In the years after the banking and thrift crisis of the 1980s and early 1990s, banking and economic conditions were favorable and relatively few banks failed. During this period, banks had record earnings but were also building up significant credit risk exposures.

Notably, between 2001 and 2008, ADC lending grew rapidly at FDIC-insured banks and, as later illustrated, shrank just as quickly as the housing bubble burst. A 2007 FDIC article on managing CRE concentrations (including ADC loans) noted that demand for CRE lending – a traditional core business for many community banks – had been strong, and a number of banks had CRE concentrations that were high by historical standards and were rising.[9] Growth in ADC lending was especially pronounced as depicted in Figure 1.

According to FDIC data, ADC lending grew 75 percent from the first quarter of 2005 to the first quarter of 2008, and ADC loan volume for all FDIC-insured banks peaked in March 2008. The FDIC's analysis of the data noted that ADC loan growth was more prevalent in (1) de novo banks; (2) small community banks; (3) certain regions of the country, such as the Southeast, Northwest, and Mountain states; and (4) states affected by the housing boom, such as Georgia, Washington, Arizona, and North Carolina.

To address the growth in CRE concentrations, the agencies issued the Joint Guidance in December 2006, which was intended to reinforce existing regulations and guidelines for real estate lending and safety and soundness. The Joint Guidance identifies institutions that are potentially exposed to significant CRE concentration risk as those that have experienced rapid growth in CRE lending, have notable exposures to a specific type of CRE, or are approaching or exceed the following supervisory criteria:

- Total loans reported for construction, land development, and other land represent 100 percent or more of the institution's total capital; or
- Total CRE loans that represent 300 percent or more of the institution's total capital, and the outstanding balance of the institution's CRE loan portfolio has increased by 50 percent or more during the prior 36 months.

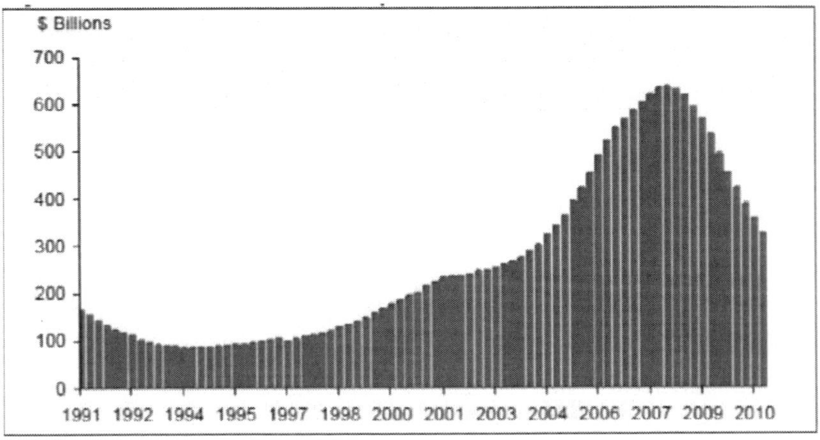

Source: FDIC's Division of Insurance and Research (DIR).

Figure 1. ADC Loans at FDIC-Supervised Institutions, 1991 to 2010.

Board and Management Oversight. If an institution has significant CRE concentration risk, its strategic plan should address the rationale for its CRE levels in relation to its overall growth objectives, financial targets, and capital. The Board of Directors (Board) should establish policy guidelines and approve an overall CRE lending strategy regarding the level and nature of CRE exposures acceptable to the institution.

Portfolio Management. Management should regularly evaluate the degree of correlation between related real estate sectors and establish internal lending guidelines and concentration limits that control the institution's overall risk exposure. Management should develop a contingency plan to reduce or mitigate concentrations in the event of adverse CRE market conditions.

Management Information Systems. A management information system should be provided to management with sufficient information to identify, measure, monitor, and manage CRE concentration risk.

Market Analysis. Market analysis should provide the institution's management and Board with information to assess whether its CRE lending strategy and policies continue to be appropriate in light of changes in CRE market conditions. An institution should perform periodic market analysis for the various property types and geographic markets represented in its portfolio.

Credit Underwriting Standards. When an institution has a CRE concentration, the establishment of sound lending policies becomes even more critical. Credit analysis should reflect both the borrower's overall creditworthiness and project-specific considerations, as appropriate.

Portfolio Stress Testing and Sensitivity Analysis. An institution with CRE concentrations should perform portfolio-level stress tests or sensitivity analysis to quantify the impact of changing economic conditions on asset quality, earnings, and capital.

Credit Risk Review Function. A strong credit risk review function is critical for an institution's self- assessment of emerging risks. An effective, accurate, and timely risk-rating system provides a foundation for the institution's credit risk review function to assess credit quality and, ultimately, to identify problem loans.

Source: Joint Guidance.

Figure 2. Key Elements Needed in a Risk Management Framework for Concentrations.

The Joint Guidance states that these criteria are not limits and are viewed neither negatively nor as a "safe harbor." According to the Joint Guidance, the ability of institutions with significant concentrations to withstand difficult market conditions will depend heavily on the adequacy of their risk management practices and capital levels. The guidance recognizes that the sophistication of an institution's risk management process will depend on the size of the CRE portfolio and the level and nature of its CRE concentration risk. Figure 2 summarizes the key elements needed for managing concentration risk as outlined in the Joint Guidance.

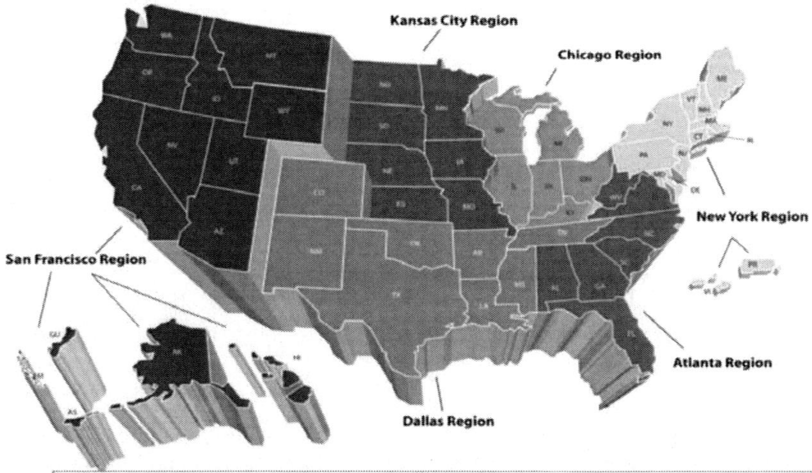

Legend

San Francisco Region • 113.8% Growth • 84 Bank Failures • $30.8 Billion in DIF Losses	Atlanta Region • 95.3% Growth • 120 Bank Failures • $24.1 Billion in DIF Losses
Chicago Region • 66% Growth • 65 Bank Failures • $10.4 Billion in DIF Losses	New York Region • 73.8% Growth • 21 Bank Failures • $7.7 Billion in DIF Losses
Dallas Region • 95.3% Growth • 25 Bank Failures • $6.1 Billion in DIF Losses	Kansas City Region • 79.5% Growth • 36 Bank Failures • $2.5 Billion in DIF Losses

Source: Office of Inspector General (OIG) analysis of data from the FDIC's Loss History Reports and Quarterly Banking Profile.

Note: Bank failure and loss data are from January 2007 to March 2011.

Figure 3. ADC Loan Growth, Bank Failures, and DIF Losses by Region.

History has demonstrated that CRE markets can experience fairly rapid changes and, by the summer of 2007, a series of complex and interrelated shocks, rooted in poor underwriting and poor administration of residential subprime mortgages and flaws in securitization practices and capital markets, began to unfold, triggering a liquidity crisis and recession. The financial crisis sparked sharp declines in real estate values in many regions of the country and set off a wave of bank failures beginning in 2008. As explained later in this report, geographic location was a factor in the degree of losses associated with CRE and ADC lending that figured prominently in many of the bank failures. Figure 3 illustrates that point and shows ADC loan growth, bank failure activity, and related DIF losses during the period covered by our review.

In response to the challenging economic conditions that began to materialize in 2007, the FDIC issued guidance in 2008 to re-emphasize the importance of strong capital and *allowance for loan and lease loss* (ALLL) levels and robust credit risk management practices for institutions with concentrated CRE exposures consistent with the Joint Guidance.

COMMON CHARACTERISTICS OF BANKS IN THIS STUDY

This section of the report discusses what we learned about the characteristics of the banks with ADC concentrations that did not fail. As noted earlier, we focused attention on a sample of 18 banks that had ADC concentrations of 300 percent or greater and were in satisfactory condition. We selected this sample, because, in our view, the experience of these 18 institutions was unique and allowed us to readily compare their practices to those institutions with ADC concentrations that failed. Notably, we did not identify a significant number of banks with high concentrations in 2007 that were in satisfactory condition in 2011. We believe this is reflective of how difficult it is for institutions with exceedingly high ADC concentrations to mitigate the concentration risk during an economic downturn. Perhaps not surprisingly, bankers we interviewed characterized the Board's and management's risk appetite to be conservative or moderate. These same bankers implemented many of the key elements of the risk management framework that regulators have said are needed to manage ADC concentrations. Additionally, a number of bankers we interviewed were quick to point out that their market areas were less impacted by the economic decline. As a result of these factors, banks in our study did not experience significant losses from their ADC portfolio and managed to maintain stable capital positions even though the economy, as a whole, experienced a steep and prolonged economic decline.

Implemented More Conservative Growth Strategies

According to the Joint Guidance, an institution's Board has ultimate responsibility for the level of risk assumed by the institution. In general, the banks that failed pursued aggressive growth strategies centered in ADC lending, which left those institutions more vulnerable to the economic downturn. While the 436 banks in our study experienced some increasing ADC concentration levels from 2005 through 2007, most of the bankers we spoke with characterized their institution's risk appetite to be conservative or moderate, and most pursued a conservative or moderate growth strategy. Bank officials from one bank explained that the bank was aggressive early but "got scared" early. The officials explained that competitive market factors influenced their decision to pursue an aggressive growth strategy in 2005 and 2006, but, overall, they tried to maintain a conservative culture and emphasize sound underwriting standards.

Figure 4 presents trend information reflecting the percentage of ADC loans to total loans for failed banks and the banks in our sample. The analysis reveals that, for the 436 banks in our study, ADC loans represented a smaller percentage of the total loan portfolio than failed banks, which reflects the Boards' lower risk appetite and ensuing strategic decisions.

Further, the 18 banks in our sample were able to significantly diversify their loan portfolio in comparison to the other banks in our study. The declining trend line for the failed banks was due to the recognition of ADC loan losses within the loan portfolio – not as a result of the banks' efforts to diversify into other loan products. Bankers we interviewed stated that once the economy declined, they mitigated the risk associated with their ADC loan concentrations by intentionally reducing their ADC loan portfolio, further diversifying their loan portfolio, and implementing pre-existing (well-developed) loan workout policies to meet the bank's increased operational demands. Most of the bank officials we spoke with from the 18 banks stated that they made conscious decisions to diversify their loan portfolio by shifting their loan mix away from ADC loans and to shrink the volume of ADC loans in response to the economic decline, which our level and trend analysis supports. A few officials acknowledged that they did not make a conscious decision to diversify or shrink their ADC loan portfolios; rather, the shift away from ADC lending happened because there was less demand for ADC loans.

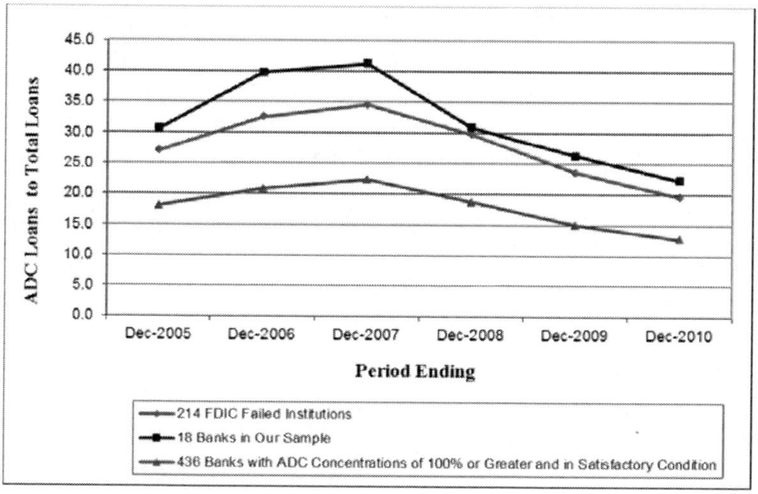

Source: OIG analysis of selected Uniform Bank Performance Report (UBPR) data.
Note: Data points presented are averages for the failed and sampled banks.

Figure 4. ADC Loans as a Percentage of Total Loans, 2005 to 2010.

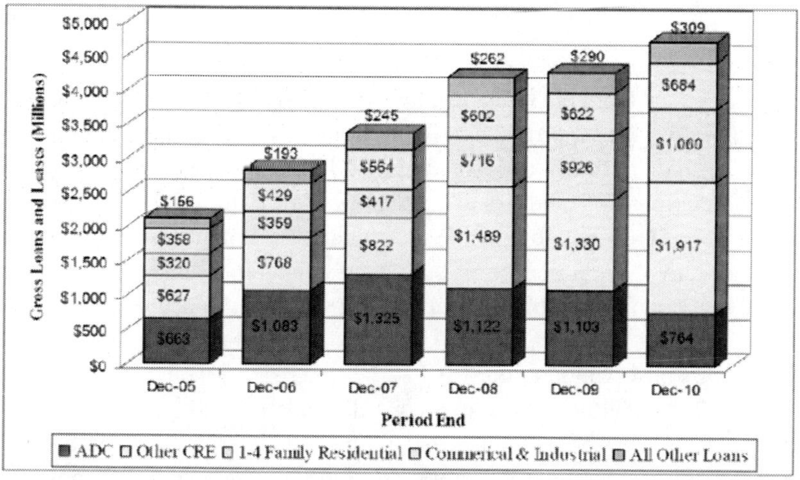

Source: OIG analysis of selected *Call Report* data.

Figure 5. Loan Portfolio Composition and Growth for the Sample of 18 Banks, 2005 to 2010.

Most officials we interviewed from the 18 banks also stated that the banks' Boards took an active role in monitoring the ADC portfolio and were familiar with the local real estate market. More than half of the bank officials from those banks stated that they relied on formal market analysis processes, including obtaining housing data and trends from third-party subscription services. The other officials we interviewed relied on less-formal processes but said they kept abreast of market conditions by maintaining strong relationships with local realtors and borrowers and being knowledgeable about their respective communities. Additionally, most of the officials from the 18 banks we interviewed stated that they proactively "ramped up" loan work-out staffing to address problem loans and did so early in the cycle. Figures 5 and 6 present loan composition and growth information for the 18 and 436 banks, respectively.

Relied on Core Deposits and Limited Net Non-Core Funding Dependence

In response to our question about funding sources, most bankers we interviewed stated they primarily relied on core deposits to fund operations and growth. Core deposits have historically been categorized as stable, less-costly deposits obtained from local customers that maintain a relationship with the institution, while brokered deposits [10] are considered potentially volatile, interest-rate-sensitive deposits from customers in search of yield. The FDIC's research indicates that core deposits may reduce a bank's probability of failure because they typically provide a bank with a stable and relatively cost-effective source of funds and are a direct indication of a bank's valuable customer relationships and franchise value. An FDIC study of core and brokered deposits noted that while examiners do not necessarily view the presence of any certain source of funding as inherently bad, the FDIC had observed that a number of bank failures occurred where concentrations in CRE and ADC lending were funded by large amounts of brokered deposits.[11] We also made this observation in our MLRs.

Figure 7 compares the net non-core dependence ratio for banks in our study and FDIC-supervised banks that failed. As illustrated, failed banks, in general, were more reliant on non-core funding sources to support their ongoing operations than were the banks in our study. The net non-core funding dependence ratio measures the extent to which a bank is using non-core funds to invest in long-term assets, which can create a liquidity concern because non-core funds can be volatile and long-term assets may not be readily converted to cash.

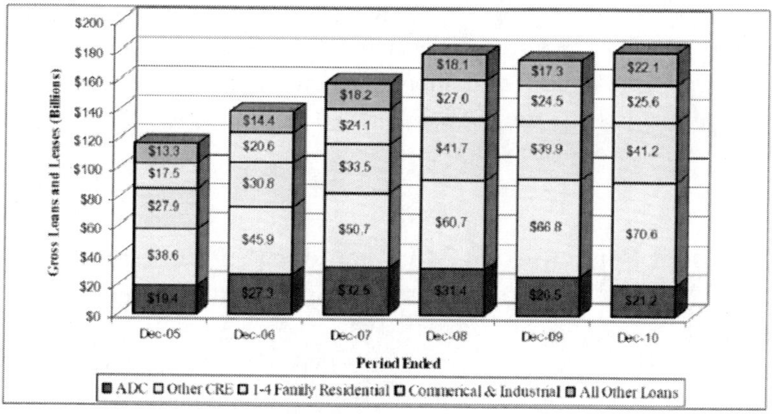

Source: OIG analysis of selected *Call Report* data.

Figure 6. Loan Portfolio Composition and Growth for 436 Banks, 2005 to 2010.

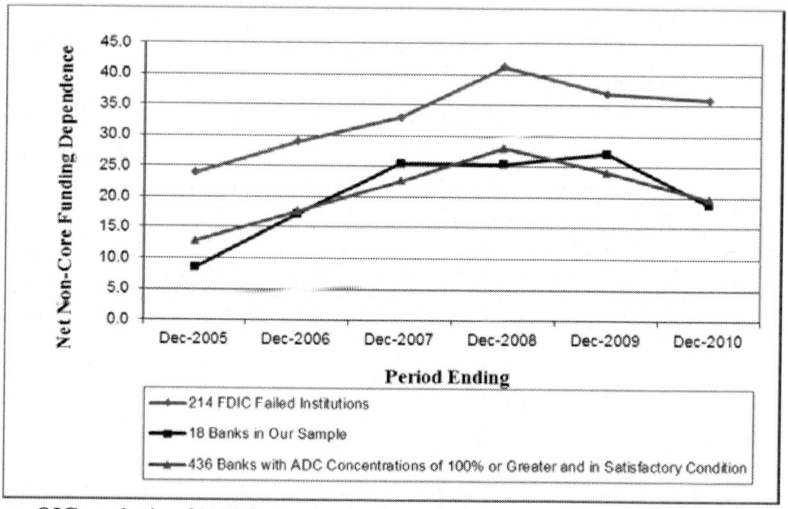

Source: OIG analysis of UBPR data.

Note: The net non-core funding dependence ratio is a bank's non-core liabilities, less short-term investments, divided by long-term assets. Data points presented are averages for failed and sampled banks.

Figure 7. Net Non-Core Funding Dependence, 2005 to 2010.

A high positive ratio may indicate a bank's possible vulnerability to adverse events in the non-core funding environment (i.e., when the cost of these funds becomes prohibitive). Further, because the failed banks entered the crisis with high levels of non-core funding, those banks had limited funding options once they became troubled or undercapitalized.[12] Conversely, banks in our study were able to utilize additional non-core funding sources to facilitate a shift or growth away from ADC lending and into other more profitable operations.

Implemented Prudent Risk Management Practices and Limited Speculative Lending, Loan Participations, and Out-of-Area Lending

In a 2010 follow-up audit report, we stated that concentrations in CRE and ADC loans, coupled with inadequate risk management practices have played a role in practically every failure that was the subject of an MLR.[13] In addition, the inappropriate use of *interest reserves* by bank management was noted in many of the MLRs we conducted. In contrast to our MLR findings, most officials we interviewed for this study characterized their bank's underwriting practices to be conservative or moderate. Further, our review of FDIC-generated underwriting survey results generally support the notion that the banks included in our study had stronger loan underwriting practices than failed banks and, consequently, a lower risk profile in general.

Long-standing supervisory guidance states that management's ability to identify, measure, monitor, and control portfolio risk through effective underwriting policies, systems, and internal controls is crucial to a sound ADC lending program.[14] The Joint Guidance reiterated that concentrations in CRE lending, coupled with weak loan underwriting and depressed CRE markets, contributed to significant credit losses in the past. According to the Joint Guidance:

- strong risk management practices are an important element of a sound CRE lending program, particularly when an institution has a concentration in CRE loans;
- financial institutions with CRE concentrations should ensure that risk management practices appropriate to the size of the portfolio, as well as the level and nature of concentrations, and the associated risk to the institution are implemented; and

- financial institutions should establish a risk management framework that effectively identifies, monitors, and controls CRE concentration risk.

In addition, FIL-22-2008, *Managing Commercial Real Estate Concentrations in a Challenging Environment*, issued March 17, 2008, provides key risk management processes for institutions with CRE concentrations, including maintaining prudent, time-tested lending policies with a strong credit review and risk rating system to identify deteriorating credit trends early and maintaining updated financial and analytical information for borrowers. For example, institutions should emphasize *global cash flow analysis* of obligors, which involves analyzing borrowers' complete financial resources and obligations. The guidance further states that inappropriately adding extra interest reserves on loans where the underlying real estate project is not performing as expected can erode collateral protection and mask loans that would otherwise be reported as delinquent.

The following paragraphs highlight the lending and underwriting and credit administration practices of banks in our study, as described by the bank officials we interviewed:

Limited or No Speculative ADC Lending. Speculative lending involves providing financing to developers for constructing homes that are not pre-sold, adding an additional dimension of risk. Monitoring a speculative single-family housing development can be especially challenging. Institutions must have a clear understanding of the demand for housing within geographic areas, submarkets, or specific projects, as well as price points within markets or projects. Most of the bankers we interviewed characterized their practices as conservative. Generally, bank officials said that speculative loans were originated only on a limited basis before the economic crisis, if at all. Further, in cases where banks did fund speculative ADC loans, bank officials indicated that loans were made to existing borrowers and were tied to strong customer relationships.

Limited or No ADC Loan Participations. *Loan participations* are a means by which banks diversify their assets and generate lending income. According to the FDIC's *Risk Management Manual of Examination Policies* (Examination Manual), a bank purchasing a participation loan is expected to perform the same degree of independent credit analysis on the loan as if the bank were the originator of the loans. To determine if a participation loan meets its credit standards, a participating bank must obtain all relevant credit information and details on collateral values, lien status, loan agreements, and participation agreements before a commitment is made to purchase. Some of our MLRs found that institutions that purchased out-of-area participations relied on the underwriting of the institution that originated the loans rather than making independent assessments of the loans prior to purchase, which was among the factors contributing to some failures. Most officials we interviewed said that their banks did not purchase loan participations or had bought participations only on a limited basis.

Limited or No Out-of-Area Lending. Out-of-area lending can diversify an institution's portfolio and reduce geographic concentration risk. However, before engaging in out-of-area lending, institutions should ensure the infrastructure is in place (i.e., staff, systems, and processes) to monitor and administer these loans. A 2010 FDIC analysis of loan underwriting data indicated that some banks increased their overall risk profiles because of this type of lending.[15] According to the FDIC's analysis, the majority (89 percent) of out-of-area lending activity was reported in commercial/CRE (including ADC) portfolios. Further, the FDIC found that institutions that exhibited frequent or common out-of-area lending activity tended to have higher levels of credit risk and more loose overall underwriting standards, particularly in ADC portfolios.

Most of the bankers we interviewed described their practices as conservative – either not originating out-of-area loans or originating these loans on a limited basis. For example, a few bank officials stated that they made an out-of-area loan to existing customers or in familiar areas. A few officials stated that they had reduced any out-of-area loan origination volume during the financial crisis.

Routine Global Cash Flow Analysis. Global cash flow analysis involves analyzing borrowers' complete financial resources and obligations. Most bankers we interviewed described their practices as conservative, stating global cash flow analysis was performed. A few officials acknowledged that they had not performed or emphasized global cash flow analysis until the economic crisis began to unfold.

Limited Use of Interest Reserve Accounts. Interest reserve accounts essentially capitalize contractual interest payments into a construction loan's principal balance, similar to the funding of other development costs that are supported by construction loan advances. The use of interest reserves in conjunction with the funding of initial development and construction costs is an acceptable lending practice subject to prudent underwriting standards, appropriate repayment terms, and the timely completion of the project in accordance with the original loan agreement. However, the use of, or over-reliance on, interest reserves beyond the timely completion of construction may be inappropriate. For example, if a project experiences delays or has diminished feasibility resulting from a weak local real estate market, interest reserves can inappropriately disguise a problem credit relationship. Most bankers we interviewed described their practices as conservative, stating that they did not originate loans with an interest reserve funding component – allowing loan proceeds to fund the borrower's interest payments.

Analysis of Loan Underwriting Survey Results. In addition to the differences highlighted above, our analysis of the FDIC's loan underwriting survey results showed that the failed banks generally took on a greater level of risk from 2004 to 2006. FDIC-supervised banks that failed also increased their risk profile more severely, as the economic cycle peaked and then began to decline in 2007, and then again in 2009. In particular, from 2004 to 2009, examiner survey results indicate that the failed banks initially had higher levels of potential risk and/or significantly increased their risk profiles above that of sound institutions, in the following areas:

- Loan growth,
- Current underwriting practices,
- Loan portfolio credit risk,
- Loan participations purchased,
- Contributions to concentrations of credit,
- Out-of-area lending,
- Loan administration risk,
- Failure to require material principal reduction before renewal,
- Lending policies differing from actual practices,
- Funding speculative residential ADC projects,
- Funding speculative commercial real estate development projects,
- Funding ADC loans without consideration of other sources of repayment (other than the project being funded),
- Funding ADC loans without consideration of the quality of other sources of repayment (when alternative sources of repayment are required),

- Failure to use realistic appraised values,
- Funding, or deferring, interest payments on ADC loans, and
- Funding 100 percent of the cost of ADC loans (land and construction) with no borrower/developer cash equity.

Survey results also indicated that in 2004, both sound and failed banks typically adjusted their loan pricing based on perceived differences in loan quality and/or risk; and to a certain extent, both populations required a material principal reduction before renewing term loans. However, as the economy began to deteriorate in 2007, and through 2009, the failed banks moved away from accurately pricing their loans based on risk and increasingly failed to require a material principal reduction before renewal.

Based on the results of the FDIC's revised examiner survey, we also noted that from October 2009 to December 2010, the failed banks continued to exhibit higher risk traits over those of sound institutions. However, the potential risk in certain areas, such as ADC loan growth and out-of-area lending, appeared to decline and/or stabilize, as banks slowed or halted originating new ADC loans. The revised examiner survey data also indicated that failed banks had higher-risk profiles than sound institutions in the following areas:

- Granting credit before obtaining a documented review or a qualified appraisal of the property;
- Liberal use of interest reserves or deferred interest payments, potentially masking rising delinquency levels;
- Weak to poor loan workout infrastructure; and
- Weak to poor credit review and grading system.

Also of note, the survey data indicated that the failed banks were typically subject to the following conditions:

- Elevated levels of concentrations in CRE loans – particularly in ADC loans,
- Weak to poor management of the CRE loan portfolio consistent with the 2006 CRE Guidance,
- Weak to poor management of CRE concentration risk,
- Very weak to distressed CRE markets,
- Declining to critically declining real estate market values, and

- An excess to a saturated supply of unsold property in the bank's real estate markets.

Generally Experienced a Lower Level of Non-Current Loans and Losses Associated with ADC Loans

In our 2010 follow-up audit report, we noted that aggressive growth centered in ADC concentrations coupled with weak risk management practices was a leading cause of losses, which led to the rapid erosion of capital during the economic downturn. The banks in our study generally experienced a lower level of non-performing loans and losses. For example, noncurrent ADC loans – loans that were 90 days or more past due or in a nonaccrual status – were significantly higher for banks that failed than the banks in our study as shown in Figure 8. An ADC lending analysis performed by the FDIC concluded that the exposure to potentially volatile real estate development markets contributed to asset quality deterioration at many institutions and, ultimately, to their failure. FDIC-generated data showed the following:

- For institutions that failed, non-performing ADC loans represented 8 percent of all non- performing assets in the first quarter of 2000 and rose to a high of 54 percent in the third quarter of 2008.
- For survivor institutions, non-performing ADC loans also rose but not as much – from almost 4 percent in the first quarter of 2000 to a decade high of 23 percent in the third quarter of 2009.
- The average non-current ratio for all loans reached a decade high of 17.61 percent at failed institutions at year-end 2010, compared with 3.02 percent among survivor institutions. The FDIC attributed the trend, in part, to the sharp rise in non-performing ADC loans.

We also looked at the ratio of net ADC loan losses to average total ADC loans, which shows the level of losses experienced within the ADC portfolio. In general, lower ratios are better because they indicate that losses for a particular loan type are a small proportion of average loans in that type. According to FDIC guidance, a high level of losses within a particular loan type may indicate underwriting, collections, or asset quality problems for that type of lending. Further, increasing trends in any type of lending indicate developing problems. Figure 9 shows that banks in our study had lower and steadier trends than banks that failed with regard to losses associated with ADC portfolios.

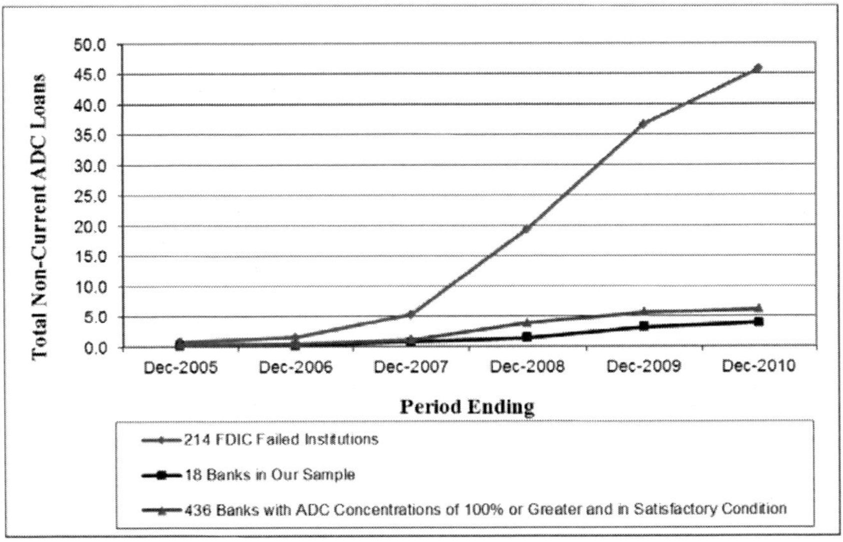

Source: OIG analysis of selected UBPR data.

Note: Data points presented are averages for failed and sampled banks.

Figure 8. Non-Current ADC Loans to Total ADC Loans, 2005 to 2010.

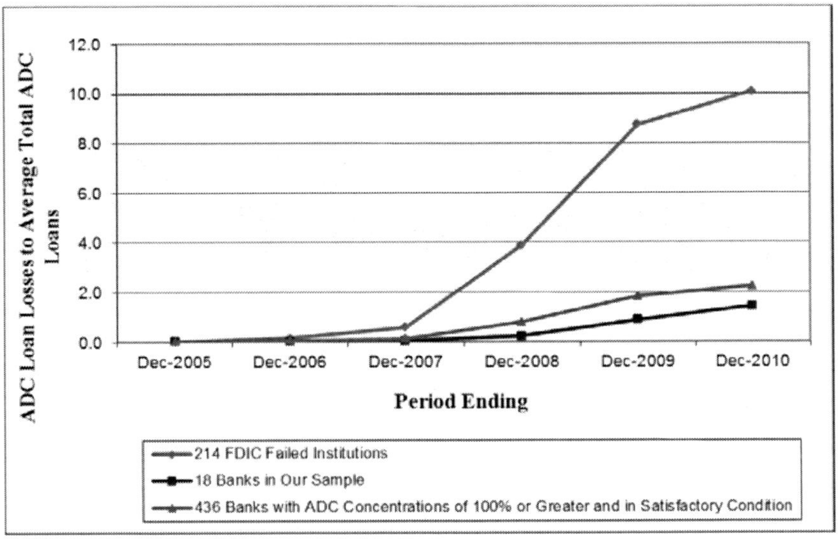

Source: OIG analysis of selected UBPR data.

Note: Data points presented are averages for failed and sampled banks.

Figure 9. Net ADC Loan Losses to Average Total ADC Loans, 2005 to 2010.

In our view, the differences in the level of losses and non-performing ADC loans between the groups can be attributed to the factors we have discussed in this report.

Maintained Stable Capital Levels and Had Access to Additional Capital If Needed

Capital serves as a buffer between operating losses and insolvency. The more capital a bank has the more losses it can withstand. In other words, a bank's capital determines the amount of time it has to correct internal weaknesses or outlast negative external influences. Generally, a bank is expected to maintain capital commensurate with the nature and extent of risks to the institution and the ability of management to identify, monitor, and control risks.

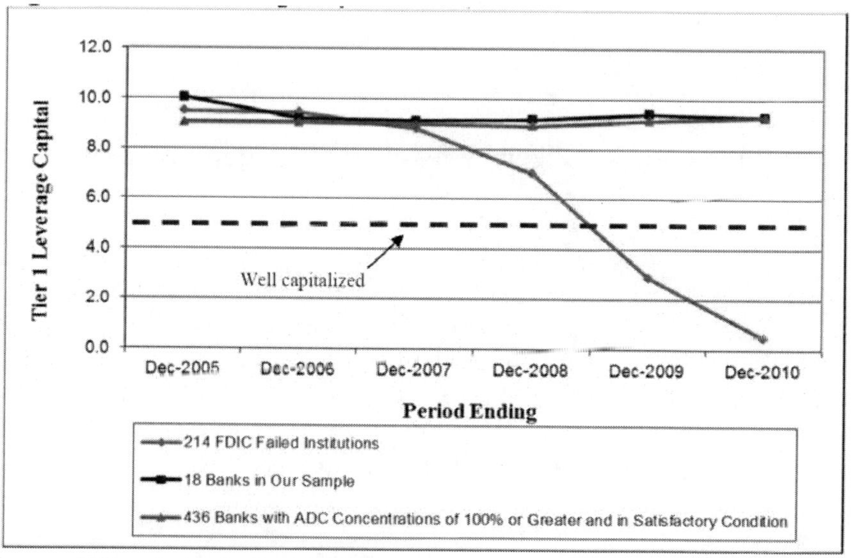

Source: OIG analysis of selected UBPR data.

Note: Data points are median ratios for failed and sampled banks. Section 38 of the FDI Act, known as Prompt Corrective Action (PCA), establishes a framework for taking prompt supervisory action against banks not adequately capitalized. Generally, a bank is considered Well Capitalized for PCA purposes if it maintains a Tier 1 Leverage Capital ratio of at least 5 percent.

Figure 10. Tier 1 Leverage Capital Ratios, 2005 to 2010.

Part 325 of the FDIC's Rules and Regulations establishes the criteria and standards the FDIC uses in calculating the minimum leverage capital (*Tier 1 (Core) Capital*) requirement and determining capital adequacy. *Risk-based capital* is another capital measure that is more explicitly and systematically sensitive to the risk profile of individual banks. A bank's risk-based capital ratio is calculated by dividing its qualifying total capital base by its risk-weighted assets. Under the risk- based framework, a bank's qualifying total capital basis consists of Tier 1 Capital and supplementary capital elements, known as *Tier 2 Capital.*

As illustrated above in Figure 9, losses associated with ADC loans were not as significant for the 436 banks in our study as the banks that failed. In the failed banks, the losses quickly eroded capital. In contrast, we found that capital positions of the 436 banks, including the 18 banks in our sample, were generally stable between 2005 and 2010 as illustrated in Figure 10. Further, most bankers commented that their bank's access to capital was not restricted—if needed, their shareholders or outside investors were willing to invest additional capital. A few bank officials explained that their bank's strong core deposit base helped to attract capital.

Geographic Location Played a Significant Role in Financial Performance

Most officials we interviewed emphasized that the bank's geographic location played a significant role in the bank's financial performance during the financial crisis. That is, the economic decline was not as steep in their marketplace as it was in some other areas of the country. Table 1 summarizes where these banks were located by FDIC region. As illustrated in Figure 3 earlier in the report, most failures occurred in the Atlanta and San Francisco regions, and only 7 of the 36 banks in our interview pool were located in those areas.

As discussed earlier in this report, although every region of the country was impacted by the financial crisis, the economic fallout was not uniform across the country. Bank failures were more concentrated in areas that experienced greater economic distress – including Georgia, Florida, Illinois, and California (as illustrated in Figure 3). Figure 11 presents the geographic location of the 18 banks in our sample.

Table 1. Location of Bankers Interviewed for Our Study

Region	Number of Banks
Atlanta	4
Chicago	2
Dallas	20
Kansas City	5
New York	2
San Francisco	3
Total	**36**

Source: OIG analysis.

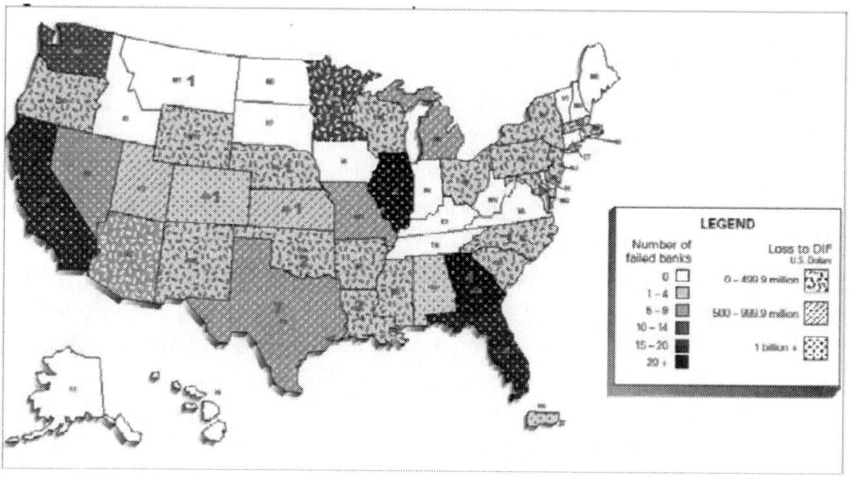

Source: OIG analysis of the FDIC's *Loss History Report.*
Note: Bank failures and losses were from January 2007 through March 2011

Figure 11. Location of the 18 Banks in Our Sample.

We found only one bank that was located in one of the states with the greatest number of failures – Georgia. Most of the 18 banks were in markets where few bank failures occurred.

SUPERVISORY APPROACH FOR TURN-AROUND BANKS

This section of the report discusses the supervisory approach for the sampled turn-around banks. We also highlight broader supervisory actions taken in response to MLR trends and other issues stemming from the recent financial crisis. We found that the supervisory approach and level of supervisory attention for the 23 turn-around banks we sampled were generally consistent with the FDIC's supervisory practices and policies and similar to the approach for banks that ultimately failed. That is, as economic conditions declined and banks' financial condition began to weaken, the FDIC's supervisory attention increased and supervisory actions were pursued. We observed that the supervisory approach yielded a better outcome – stable or improved examination ratings – because of managements' responsiveness in addressing supervisory concerns.

Examination Findings Were Similar to Those for Failed Banks

The *FDIC's supervision program* primarily relies on annual onsite examinations and its *offsite review program* to monitor the condition of its banks. The onsite examinations provide information necessary to understand the nature, relative seriousness, and ultimate cause of a bank's problems, and thus assist in providing a factual foundation on which to base corrective measures, recommendations, and instructions.[16] The FDIC's offsite review program is designed to identify emerging supervisory concerns and potential problems so that supervisory strategies can be adjusted appropriately. For instance, offsite reviews may trigger targeted visitations.

To understand the supervisory history of each of the 23 turn-around banks, we reviewed examination reports for these banks from 2007 through 2011.[17] Although examiners identified some weaknesses, they generally considered the turn-around banks' risk management practices to be adequate before the financial crisis. ADC concentrations were generally noted to be a risk in the 2008 and 2009 examinations, as losses within the portfolio materialized. In addition, we noted that examiners generally determined that the methodology and funding for the ALLL was inadequate during the same period. As discussed in the next section of this report, examiners downgraded composite and component ratings and pursued enforcement actions against the banks to address supervisory concerns. Further, targeted visitations were performed as warranted.

As discussed in our 2010 follow-up audit report related to supervisory program enhancements, the CAMELS rating for failed financial institutions placed greater emphasis on a bank's financial condition at the time of the examination and levels of capital and earnings, rather than the bank's ability to successfully mitigate identified risks. As such, with the benefit of hindsight, we often concluded in our MLR reports that greater supervisory concern and more timely supervisory action may have been prudent. Further, in some cases, MLR reports noted that doing so would generally have served to establish supervisory expectations and prompted Boards and management to implement corrective actions to address supervisory concerns. Although the supervisory approach proved effective, we believe that earlier emphasis on risk management practices at the turn-around banks would have been equally beneficial.

Enforcement Actions Addressing Asset Quality, Capital, and Management Were Imposed as Banks' Financial Condition Deteriorated – Generally Consistent with the Approach for Failed Banks

In general, supervisory attention is heightened when banks are in a less-than-satisfactory condition. Accordingly, the FDIC uses formal and informal enforcement actions to address practices, conditions, or violations that could result in risk of loss or damage to a financial institution. Specifically, to assure greater uniformity of action and help assure that supervisory efforts are directed to banks most in need, the FDIC's examination policy presumes either a formal or informal administrative action will be taken on banks with 3, 4, or 5 composite CAMELS ratings unless specific circumstances argue strongly to the contrary. A composite 3 rating implies that a bank has weaknesses that, if not corrected, could worsen. Informal actions are generally appropriate for institutions that receive a composite 3 rating. The FDIC may recommend that the bank's Directors adopt a *Bank Board Resolution* (BBR), which establishes the bank's commitment to address specific deficiencies. Alternatively, the FDIC may enter into a *Memorandum of Understanding* (MOU) with the institutions.

Banks with composite ratings of 4 or 5 will, by definition, have problems of sufficient severity to warrant formal action. In these cases, the FDIC will typically take formal action pursuant to section 8 of the FDI Act against all insured state nonmember banks rated 4 or 5, where evidence of unsafe or unsound practices is present. Exceptions to the policy may be considered when the condition of the bank clearly reflects significant improvement resulting from an effective corrective program or where individual circumstances strongly mitigate the appropriateness or feasibility of this supervisory tool. For example, acceptable action by the state authority might preempt the need for

FDIC action, or qualified new management might allow the use of an MOU instead of a formal *consent order*.

We found that each of the 23 turn-around banks was subject to some type of formal and/or informal action between 2007 and 2010 and, as such, heightened supervisory attention consistent with the FDIC's policies. In total, the turn-around banks were subject to a total of 42 FDIC stipulated (i.e., agreed to) actions. We determined the timeliness of actions was consistent with broader trends for enforcement actions issued during the period. Specifically, we found as the economy deteriorated, the number of actions issued per year for all FDIC-supervised banks dramatically increased, rising to 1,127 actions during 2010. From 2005 through 2010, the FDIC and/or state regulatory authorities issued (or assumed responsibility for) approximately 3,213 enforcement actions. Figure 12 shows the trend with respect to enforcement actions during this period, while Figure 13 shows selected categories of actions taken.

For the turn-around banks, the 42 FDIC-stipulated enforcement actions included a total of 558 provisions. In general, the actions routinely included provisions that addressed capital, asset quality, management, earnings, and reserves. For example, a capital provision was included in 90 percent (38 of 42) of the enforcement actions. The capital-related provisions required the bank to increase and/or maintain capital at a specific targeted ratio. Eighty-eight percent of the actions also included an asset quality-related provision. These provisions typically required an institution to charge off non-performing loans, develop a plan for reducing classified assets, and improve loan underwriting and loan administration. In addition, 98 percent (41 of 42) of enforcement actions included provisions requiring the banks to assess and improve or obtain qualified management. Each of the enforcement actions also included a provision requiring the turn-around banks to submit quarterly progress reports, which are a common tool the FDIC uses to monitor institutions operating under an enforcement action. The FDIC usually conducted on-site visitations between full-scope examinations to monitor these institutions' progress in addressing critical weaknesses.

As reflected in the improved composite ratings, most of the turn-around banks took steps to substantially comply with supervisory actions and address problem areas, including raising or securing additional capital, as needed. In most cases, examiners noted management's substantial compliance with provisions in the subsequent examination. We noted that in some cases, the injection of capital was accompanied by a change of management control. These two factors were likely contributors to improvements noted by examiners, and the additional capital allowed the existing or new management team the time necessary to implement corrective actions. Although the condition of banks had improved, most banks remained subject to an enforcement action and heightened supervisory attention as of April 2011. In some cases, formal orders were removed and replaced by informal actions.

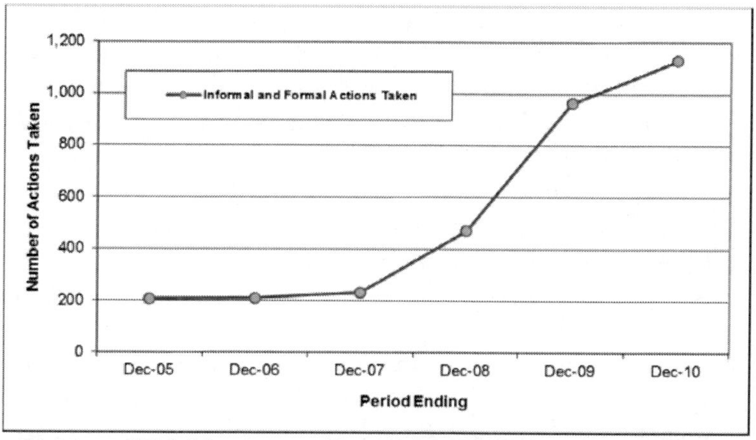

Source: Division of Risk Management Supervision (RMS) Formal and Informal Action Tracking (FIAT) System.

Figure 12. Trend Analysis of Enforcement Actions, 2005 to 2010.

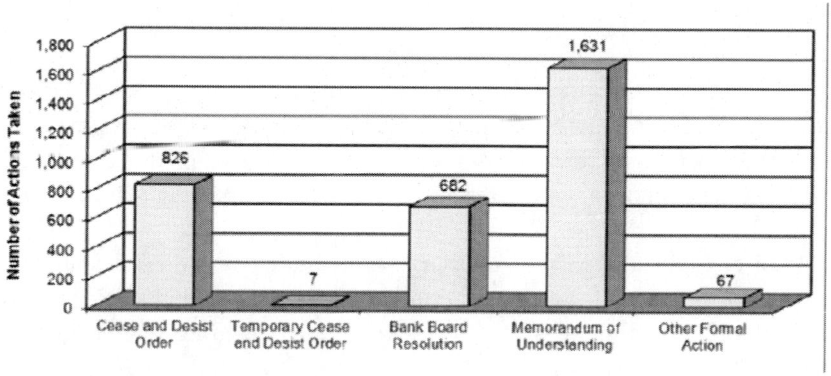

Source: RMS FIAT System.

Note: The figure does not include civil money penalties, orders for removal or investigation, or certain other actions. The *Other Formal Action* category primarily includes state-issued actions that the FDIC did not sign.

Figure 13. Selected Categories of Enforcement Actions, 2005 to 2010.

The FDIC Has Taken Steps to Address Specific MLR Trends and Issues

In response to MLR findings and other issues, the FDIC has issued specific examiner and financial institution guidance, as discussed in our 2010 report. Briefly, actions taken included:

- Establishing the importance of implementing a forward-looking approach to examinations and reflecting financial institution risks in the assigned CAMELS rating as part of its *Forward-Looking Training Initiative*;
- Recognizing factors that are indicative of elevated risk associated with management, which included high-risk appetite and degree of responsiveness to examiner recommendations;
- Issuing additional guidance regarding the inappropriate use of interest reserves;
- Emphasizing to examiners the risks that the use of non-core funding can present to a financial institution;
- Issuing guidance regarding the consideration of brokered deposits in the deposit insurance risk assessment process, use of such funding sources for institutions that are in a weakened condition, processing requests for brokered deposit waivers, and interest rate restrictions for banks that are less than *Well Capitalized*;
- Issuing guidance to emphasize the importance of monitoring institutions subject to enforcement actions, including the need to clarify expectations for quarterly progress reports, meet with an institution's Board at the beginning of a corrective program, and conduct onsite supervisory activities between examinations; and
- Enhancing off-site monitoring activities for various high-risk issues.

As discussed earlier in this report, the Joint Guidance addresses sound risk management practices for concentrations in CRE lending (and ADC lending) and reinforces existing regulations for real estate lending and safety and soundness.

As the financial crisis was unfolding, the FDIC issued additional CRE- and ADC-related guidance during 2008 and 2009 and has implemented a number of other initiatives to ensure examiners have the tools necessary to assess an institution's vulnerability with regard to concentrations.

Banking Officials Had Positive Views of the Examination Process, but Concerns Exist Regarding Examiner Review of CRE Lending and Regulatory Burden

Most bankers characterized the examination process as "good" or "okay" and viewed the examination process as beneficial. Also, most bankers viewed the Joint Guidance positively, explaining that the guidance helped to raise their own awareness or reinforced the need for good credit administration and underwriting practices even if their practices were in line with the guidance. A few bankers offered a different perspective, commenting that the guidance was issued too late to be fully effective. Further, a few bankers stated that the guidance has prompted examiners to be overly critical of concentrations. For example, a few bankers stated that examiners were treating supervisory thresholds as limits, which is inconsistent with the guidance.

In a related vein, GAO completed a study of examiners' practices related to CRE lending in May 2011.[18] The scope of GAO's report included institutions with CRE concentrations of 300 percent or greater and CAMELS ratings of 3, 4, and 5, which provided for a broader range of views than our study. Based on interviews with officials from the 43 banks in its sample, GAO reported that banking officials' overarching concern was that examiners were applying CRE guidance more stringently than before the financial crisis. Banking officials also informed GAO that:

- Examiners were classifying loans that were technically performing based on a global cash flow analysis of the borrower's ability to repay the loan. Such an analysis would show that even though a borrower is currently paying a CRE loan, the borrower's income and other debt obligations, when reviewed as a whole, raised questions about whether the borrower could continue paying the CRE loan in the future.
- Examiners were being more critical of recent appraisals. For example, according to some of the officials GAO interviewed, examiners have been requiring appraisals on CRE collateral more often, criticizing the banks' appraisal review process, and criticizing the appraisals themselves.
- Examiners were misapplying the 2006 Joint Guidance and viewing the 300 percent CRE concentration threshold as a lending limit, even though the Joint Guidance states that the CRE and ADC concentration levels are thresholds that may warrant greater supervisory scrutiny.

- Examiners were critically assessing the management component rating and basing the rating on asset quality and other component ratings as well as portfolio deterioration due to the broader economic downturn, which was out of the bankers' control.

GAO noted that a few bankers they interviewed considered that the additional scrutiny was appropriate given the current CRE market situation and the severity of the economic downturn. GAO recommended that the federal banking regulators enhance or supplement the Joint Guidance to ensure the guidance was consistently applied.

In January 2012, the Congress passed, and the President signed, legislation requiring our office to study, among other things, examiner implementation of appraisal and CRE loan workout guidance. We will be providing a written report to the Congress no later than January 2013 that will address the views of the bankers discussed above.

Finally, while not related to supervision of ADC concentrations, most bankers that we interviewed expressed concerns about the level of regulatory burden associated with the Dodd-Frank Act, particularly newly established compliance-related regulations for smaller banks. Because this issue was raised by most of the bankers we interviewed, we followed up and noted that many of the issues have been discussed as part of the FDIC Advisory Committee on Community Banking, which provides the FDIC with advice and guidance on a broad range of important policy issues impacting small community banks throughout the country. Advisory committee minutes noted that FDIC officials have acknowledged the burdens that new regulations impose on community banks and have observed that every new regulation imposes an incremental cost to community banks that is higher than the cost to large banks. The minutes also reflect that FDIC officials were sensitive to the fact that the new regulations address issues that arose with large banks and that the FDIC needs to avoid unintended trickle-down effects on community banks. Further, FDIC officials recognized that even though many of the new rules do not impact community banks, significant effort is often required to sort through the many publications in order for banks to make that determination.

Observations and Matters for Consideration

Prior to the recent financial crisis, competition among financial institutions for growth, profitability, and community influence often resulted in the compromise of sound credit principles and acquisition of unsound loans. Ultimately, that type of compromise resulted in a spate of bank failures not seen since the 1980s—a period that, in broad terms, was not that long ago. Much was written following the banking crisis of the 1980s and early 1990s, and there were ample discussions of lessons learned.

In addition, far-reaching legislative and regulatory actions were taken and extensive guidance was issued by regulators on key risks, including repeated warnings and references to best practices related to ADC lending because it is a highly specialized field with inherent risks that must be managed and controlled.

Nevertheless, unlike the circumstances at the banks we studied, Boards and management at too many other institutions pursued profits through growth and higher earning, risky assets, in an era of easy credit, while lacking robust risk management practices—a story that appears very similar to the one told just over 20 years ago.

We found some institutions with ADC concentrations were able to weather the recent financial crisis without experiencing a corresponding decline in their overall financial condition. The factors that contributed to their survival validate the point that regulators have emphasized and reiterated for years – a well-informed and active Board, strong management, sound credit administration and underwriting practices, and adequate capital are important to managing ADC concentrations in a safe and sound manner. In addition, the banks in our study did not rely on brokered deposits to fund growth, and geographic location factored into the degree of ADC loan losses.

Ultimately, the strategic decisions and disciplined, values-based practices and actions taken by the Boards and management helped to mitigate and control the institutions' overall ADC loan risk exposure and allowed them to react to a changing economic environment. Unlike many failed banks that saw their capital evaporate rapidly because of the losses associated with their ADC portfolios, the banks in our study experienced comparatively fewer losses and were able to maintain stable capital positions.

Further, we determined that the FDIC's supervisory approach and level of supervisory attention for the turn-around banks were generally consistent with the FDIC's supervisory practices and policies and similar to that of failed banks. In that regard, the following areas in which the FDIC has implemented revised supervisory policies and procedures are worth highlighting.

- While the supervisory approach we observed for turn-around banks proved effective, similar to observations made in our MLRs, we believe that earlier emphasis on risk management practices would have been beneficial. To that end, the Corporation completed a training initiative in 2010 for its entire supervisory workforce that focused on placing greater emphasis on risk management practices for institutions with elevated risk profiles. The training addressed the importance of considering management practices as well as current financial performance or trends when assigning ratings, consistent with existing examination guidance. This approach encourages bank management to continuously implement effective risk management practices and examiners to promptly address control weaknesses, regardless of how well a bank is performing financially.

- Management's responsiveness to supervisory concerns was a key differentiating factor between banks that failed and turn-around banks that we reviewed. Generally, our MLRs have shown that examiners identified significant risks but did not take timely and effective action to address those risks until the bank had started to experience significant financial deterioration in the loan or investment portfolios. In response to those findings, the FDIC has conducted training and issued guidance aimed at timely communication of risks to financial institutions, prompt supervisory and enforcement actions, and examiner follow- up. The Corporation should remain vigilant in ensuring that its processes and examiners sufficiently promote prompt and effective responses to examination findings and supervisory actions, including timely and progressive enforcement of situations involving banks that are not responsive to examination findings, repeat criticisms, or violations.

Finally, the FDIC has to date, and must continue to make certain, that lessons learned associated with ADC concentrations become ingrained in day-to-day supervisory activities and greater emphasis on risk management practices for institutions with elevated risk profiles is sustained regardless of the health of the economy or banking industry or the political appetite for financial regulation.

We trust that the analysis and conclusions of our study will benefit the Corporation and assist in management's continual efforts to have an efficient and effective supervisory program that protects depositors and the DIF.

CORPORATION RESPONSE

We provided a draft of this report to RMS on August 9, 2012. The FDIC was not required to provide a written response because the report contained no recommendations, and management opted to only provide informal comments regarding the technical accuracy of certain report content. We made changes to the report, where appropriate, to address those comments. RMS did express general agreement with the evaluation results at the exit conference for this assignment.

APPENDIX 1. OBJECTIVE, SCOPE, AND METHODOLOGY

Objective and Scope

The objective of this evaluation was to study the characteristics and supervisory approaches for FDIC-supervised institutions that had significant ADC loan concentrations in December 2007 and were not considered to be problem banks as of April 2011.

We performed our evaluation work from July 2011 through February 2012 in accordance with the Council of the Inspectors General on Integrity and Efficiency's *Quality Standards for Inspection and Evaluation*.

Methodology

To identify the population of banks relevant to our study, we stratified data associated with the 4,535 FDIC-supervised banks, using the ratio of ADC loans to total capital as of December 2007 and the composite CAMELS rating as of April 8, 2011. The ratio of ADC and CRE loans to capital provides the basis of supervisory thresholds that were established in the Joint Guidance. Table 2 provides a stratification of FDIC-supervised banks by ADC loan concentration levels and condition, as defined earlier in the report by their CAMELS rating.

We focused our analysis on the following:

- Institutions with 100 percent or greater ADC concentrations and in satisfactory condition. We identified 436 institutions meeting our criteria. We focused particular attention on a sample of 18 institutions in this group that had ADC concentrations of 300 percent or greater.

- Institutions meeting our turn-around criteria. That is, institutions with concentrations between 100 percent and 300 percent that were in less-than-satisfactory condition during our scope period and received a higher composite rating as of April 2011. We identified 71 institutions meeting our criteria and selected a non-statistical sample of 23 banks to study the FDIC's supervisory approach.

None of the sampling techniques that we used can be used to project to the intended population by standard statistical methods.

We took a three-pronged approach to perform this study:

Discussions with bank officials. We contacted bank officials from 38 institutions, comprised of (1) 28 of the 436 institutions, including officials from the 18 banks in our sample and (2) 10 randomly selected banks from our pool of turn-around banks. Thirty-six officials agreed to talk with us.

Using structured interviewed questions, we asked the bankers to:

- Describe their respective lending and growth strategies and how they were able to mitigate the risk associated with the ADC loan concentrations;
- The extent to which local market conditions or geographic location impacted the bank's financial performance during the financial crisis;
- Characterize their loan underwriting and credit administration practices as liberal, moderate, or conservative;
- Describe their ability to raise capital; and
- Identify any lessons learned.

We also solicited their views on the FDIC's supervision as related to CRE and ADC concentrations.

Throughout the report, when we summarize statements about the 36 banks for which we interviewed associated officials, we use the term "few" to refer to 1-9 of 36 bankers making the statement, "some" to refer to 10-24 of 36 bankers making the statement; and "most" to refer to 25-36 bankers making the statement. We do not provide specific numbers in the body of the report to avoid overstating the precision of the results.

Table 2. Stratification of FDIC-Supervised Banks by ADC Loan Concentration

ADC Loans to Total Capital	No Rating*	Satisfactory Condition	Less-Than- Satisfactory Condition	Total
100% percent or greater		436	738	1,174
Less than 100%	5	2,627	729	3,361
Total	**5**	**3,063**	**1,467**	**4,535**

Source: OIG analysis based on data available through RMS's Virtual Supervisory Information on the Net (ViSION).

* A rating was not assigned to these institutions at the analysis based on data available through RMS's ViSION.

Analysis and comparison of financial and other data. Using data from UBPRs, we performed level and trend analysis that compared and contrasted the key financial performance ratios for banks in our population with the 214 FDIC-supervised institutions that failed between January 2007 and April 2011. The UBPR is produced quarterly from Call Report data submitted by banks.

We also obtained loan survey results from DIR and RMS in order to compare and contrast the loan survey results using the FDIC's survey results from January 2007 to December 2010. We used data from the *Underwriting Survey Questionnaire* and the *Credit and Consumer Products/Services Survey*. The *Credit and Consumer Products/Services Survey* replaced the *Underwriting Survey Questionnaire* in 2009 to strengthen the identification and tracking of risks facing insured institutions. These surveys are completed by examiners at FDIC-supervised banks.

Evaluation of the FDIC's supervisory strategy. To study the FDIC's supervisory approach we reviewed supervisory information available for our sample of 23 turn-around banks. For each bank, we obtained and reviewed key supervisory documents from 2007 through 2011, including completed reports of examination, *problem bank memoranda*, and information from the FDIC's ViSION system, including summary-related information and information about enforcement actions taken.

Our basic understanding of risks associated with CRE/ADC concentrations is based on our review of FDIC policies, regulatory guidance, and various CRE/ADC-related reports from the GAO and the FDIC as noted throughout the report. We also reviewed MLR reports issued by our office from January 2007 through March 2011 and other studies written on the causes of the bank failures during the recent financial crisis to provide a general context for the role CRE/ADC concentrations played in the failures.

APPENDIX 2. GLOSSARY

Acquisition, Development, and Construction (ADC) Loans	ADC loans are a component of CRE that provide funding for acquiring and developing land for future construction and that provide interim financing for residential or commercial structures.
Allowance for Loan and Lease Losses (ALLL)	The ALLL is an estimate of uncollectible amounts that is used to reduce the book value of loans and leases to the amount that is expected to be collected. It is established in recognition that some loans in the institution's overall loan and lease portfolio will not be repaid. Boards of Directors are responsible for ensuring that their institutions have controls in place to consistently determine the allowance in accordance with the institutions' stated policies and procedures, generally accepted accounting principles, and supervisory guidance.
Bank Board Resolution (BBR)	A BBR is an informal commitment adopted by a financial institution's Board of Directors (often at the request of the FDIC) directing the institution's personnel to take corrective action regarding specific noted deficiencies. A BBR may also be used as a tool to strengthen and monitor the institution's progress with regard to a particular component rating or activity.
Call Report	Reports of Condition and Income, often referred to as Call Reports, include basic financial data for insured commercial banks in the form of a balance sheet, an income statement, and supporting schedules. According to the Federal Financial Institutions Examination Council's (FFIEC) instructions for preparing Call Reports, national banks, state member banks, and insured nonmember banks are required to

submit a Call Report to the FFIEC's Central Data Repository (an Internet-based system used for data collection) as of the close of business on the last day of each calendar quarter.

Commercial Real Estate (CRE) Loans CRE loans are land development and construction loans (including 1-4 family residential and commercial construction loans) and other land loans. CRE loans also include loans secured by multifamily property and nonfarm nonresidential property, where the primary source of repayment is derived from rental income associated with the property or the proceeds of the sale, refinancing, or permanent financing of the property.

Concentration A concentration is a significantly large volume of economically related assets that an institution has advanced or committed to a certain industry, person, entity, or affiliated group. These assets may, in the aggregate, present a substantial risk to the safety and soundness of the institution.

Consent Order A formal enforcement action issued by a financial institution regulator to a bank or affiliated party to stop an unsafe or unsound practice or a violation of laws and regulations. A consent order may be terminated when the bank's condition has significantly improved and the action is no longer needed or the bank has materially complied with its terms

De novo bank A de novo bank is a newly established bank that is in its first 7 years of operation. De novo banks are subject to additional supervisory oversight and regulatory controls, including the development and maintenance of a current business plan and increased examination frequency.

FDIC's Supervision Program The FDIC's supervision program promotes the safety and soundness of FDIC-supervised institutions, protects consumers' rights, and promotes community investment initiatives by FDIC-supervised institutions. The FDIC's RMS (1) performs examinations of FDIC-supervised institutions to assess their overall financial condition, management policies and practices (including internal control systems), and compliance with applicable laws and regulations and (2) issues related guidance to institutions and examiners.

Global Cash Flow Analysis A global cash flow analysis is a comprehensive evaluation of borrower capacity to perform on a loan. During underwriting, proper global cash flow must thoroughly analyze projected cash flow and guarantor support. Beyond the individual loan, global cash flow must consider all other relevant factors, including: guarantor's related debt at other financial institutions, future economic conditions, as well as obtaining current and complete operating statements of all related entities. In addition, global cash flow analysis should be routinely conducted as a part of credit administration. The extent and frequency of global cash flow analysis should be commensurate to the amount of risk associated with the particular loan.

Interest Reserve Account An interest reserve account allows a lender to periodically advance loan funds to pay interest charges on the outstanding balance of the loan. The interest is capitalized and added to the loan balance. Frequently, ADC loan budgets will include an interest reserve to carry the project from origination to completion and may cover the project's anticipated sellout or lease-up period.

Loan Participation The transfer of an undivided interest in all or part of the principal amount of a loan from a seller, known as the "lead," to a buyer, known as the "participant," without recourse to the lead, pursuant to an agreement between the lead and the participant. "Without recourse" means that the loan participation is not subject to any agreement that requires the lead to repurchase the participant's interest or to otherwise compensate the participant upon the borrower's default on the underlying loan.

Material Loss As defined by section 38(k)(2)(B) of the FDI Act, a loss is material if it exceeds the greater of $25 million or 2 percent of an institution's total assets at the time the FDIC was appointed as the receiver. The Dodd-Frank Wall Street Reform and Consumer Protection Act amended section 38(k) of the FDI Act in part by increasing the MLR threshold from $25 million to $200 million for losses that occur for the period January 1, 2010 through December 31, 2011, and to $150 million for failures occurring during 2012 and 2013.

Memorandum of Understanding (MOU)	An MOU is an informal agreement between the institution and the FDIC, which is signed by both parties. The State Authority may also be party to the agreement. MOUs are designed to address and correct identified weaknesses in an institution's condition.
Offsite Review Program	The FDIC's offsite review program is designed to identify emerging supervisory concerns and potential problems so that supervisory strategies can be adjusted appropriately. Offsite reviews are performed quarterly for each bank that appears on the Offsite Review List. Regional management is responsible for implementing procedures to ensure that offsite review findings are factored into examination schedules and other supervisory activities.
Problem Bank Memorandum	A problem bank memorandum documents the FDIC's concerns with an institution and the corrective action in place or to be implemented and is used to effect interim rating changes on the FDIC's systems.
Prompt Corrective Action (PCA)	The purpose of PCA is to resolve the problems of insured depository institutions at the least possible long-term cost to the DIF. Part 325, subpart B, of the FDIC Rules and Regulations, 12 Code of Federal Regulations, section 325.101, et, seq., implements section 38, *Prompt Corrective Action*, of the FDI Act, 12 United States Code section 1831(o), by establishing a framework for determining capital adequacy and taking supervisory actions against depository institutions that are in an unsafe or unsound

condition. The following terms are used to describe capital adequacy: (1) *Well Capitalized*, (2) *Adequately Capitalized*, (3) *Undercapitalized*, (4) *Significantly Undercapitalized*, and (5) *Critically Undercapitalized.*

Provision Specific corrective measures an institution or individual respondent is required to take under a corrective action.

Risk-Based Capital A "supplemental" capital standard under Part 325 of the FDIC Rules and Regulations. Under the risk-based framework, a bank's qualifying total capital base consists of two types of capital elements, "core capital" (Tier 1) and "supplementary capital" (Tier 2).

Tier 1 (Core) Capital Defined in Part 325 of the FDIC Rules and Regulations, 12 Code of Federal
Regulations, section 325.2(v), as:

The sum of:

- Common stockholder's equity (common stock and related surplus, undivided profits, disclosed capital reserves, foreign currency translation adjustments, less net unrealized losses on available-for-sale securities with readily determinable market values);
- Non-cumulative perpetual preferred stock; and
- Minority interest in consolidated subsidiaries;

Minus:

- Certain intangible assets;
- Identified losses;
- Investments in securities subsidiaries subject to section 337.4; and
- Deferred tax assets in excess of the limit set forth in section 325.5(g).

Tier 2 (Supplemental) Capital Tier 2 capital is defined in Appendix A to Part 325 of the FDIC Rules and Regulations and is generally the sum of:

- Allowances for loan and lease losses, up to a maximum of 1.25 percent of risk-weighted assets;
- Cumulative perpetual preferred stock, long-term

preferred stock. and related surplus;
- Perpetual preferred stock (dividend is reset periodically);
- Hybrid capital instruments; and
- Term subordinated debt and intermediate-term preferred stock.

Uniform Bank Performance Report (UBPR)	The UBPR is an individual analysis of financial institution financial data and ratios that includes extensive comparisons to peer group performance. The report is produced by the FFIEC for the use of banking supervisors, bankers, and the general public and is produced quarterly from Call Report data submitted by banks.
Uniform Financial Institutions Rating System (UFIRS)	Financial institution regulators and examiners use the UFIRS to evaluate a bank's performance in six components represented by the CAMELS acronym: **C**apital adequacy, **A**sset quality, **M**anagement practices, **E**arnings performance, **L**iquidity position, and **S**ensitivity to market risk. Each component, and an overall composite score, is assigned a rating of 1 through 5, with 1 having the least regulatory concern and 5 having the greatest concern.
Wholesale Funding	Wholesale funding sources include, but are not limited to, federal funds, public funds, Federal Home Loan Bank advances, the Federal Reserve's primary credit program, foreign deposits, brokered deposits, and deposits obtained through the Internet or certificate of deposit listing services. Financial institutions may use wholesale funding sources as an alternative to core deposits to satisfy funding and liability management needs.

APPENDIX 3. ACRONYMS

ADC	Acquisition, Development, and Construction
ALLL	Allowance for Loan and Lease Losses
BBR	Bank Board Resolution

CAMELS	**C**apital Adequacy, **A**sset Quality, **M**anagement Practices, **E**arnings Performance, **L**iquidity Position, and **S**ensitivity to Market Risk
CRE	Commercial Real Estate
DIF	Deposit Insurance Fund
DIR	Division of Insurance and Research
FDI	Federal Deposit Insurance
FFIEC	Federal Financial Institutions Examination Council
FIAT	Formal and Informal Action Tracking
FIL	Financial Institution Letter
GAO	Government Accountability Office
MLR	Material Loss Review
MOU	Memorandum of Understanding
OIG	Office of Inspector General
PCA	Prompt Corrective Action
RMS	Division of Risk Management Supervision
UBPR	Uniform Bank Performance Report
UFIRS	Uniform Financial Institutions Rating System
ViSION	Virtual Supervisory Information on the Net

End Notes

[1] Throughout this report, we use the terms "FDIC-supervised institution" and "bank" interchangeably unless noted otherwise.

[2] Underlined terms are defined in the Glossary, Appendix 2.

[3] For purposes of this report, banks with 1 or 2 CAMELS composite ratings were considered to be in satisfactory condition and banks with 3, 4, or 5 ratings were considered to be in less than satisfactory condition. Financial institution regulators and examiners use the *Uniform Financial Institutions Rating System* (UFIRS) to evaluate a bank's performance in six components represented by the CAMELS acronym – Capital adequacy, **A**sset quality, **M**anagement practices, **E**arnings performance, **L**iquidity position, and **S**ensitivity to market risk – and determine an overall composite rating.

[4] The guidance was issued jointly by the Office of the Comptroller of the Currency, the Board of Governors of the Federal Reserve System, and the FDIC in December 2006.

[5] Level analysis is the process of reviewing financial statement ratios and volumes as of a specific date. Level analysis allows for a comparison of performance. Trend analysis is the process of assessing the general direction or prevailing tendency (i.e., increasing, decreasing, or stable) of operating ratios or volumes over several periods (i.e., generally over a 5-year period) using the level of each period.

[6] A non-statistical sample is judgmental and cannot be projected to the intended population by standard statistical methods. See Appendix 1 for a detailed description of the sampling methodology used during the audit.

[7] Appendix 1 provides information about how we use these terms.

[8] As required by section 38(k) of the Federal Deposit Insurance (FDI) Act, as amended by the Dodd-Frank Wall Street Reform and Consumer Protection Act (Dodd-Frank Act), when the DIF incurs a material loss, the IG of the appropriate federal banking agency is required to make a written report to that agency. The report is to consist of a review of the agency's supervision of the institution and a determination as to why the institution's problems resulted in a material loss to the DIF and recommendations to prevent future losses.

[9] FDIC Supervisory Insights, *Managing Commercial Real Estate Concentrations,* Winter 2007.

[10] Brokered deposits are a type of *wholesale funding.*

[11] Pursuant to section 1506 of the Dodd-Frank Act, the FDIC completed the *Study on Core Deposits and Brokered Deposits* (July 8, 2011).

[12] Section 29 of the FDI Act and Part 337.6 of the FDIC Rules and Regulations address restrictions placed on financial institutions that are deemed to be less than *Well Capitalized* for *Prompt Corrective Action* purposes, including the use of brokered deposits and interest-rate restrictions.

[13] FDIC OIG report entitled, *Follow-up Audit of FDIC Supervision Program Enhancements,* dated December 23, 2010, (Report No. MLR 11-010).

[14] *Internal and Regulatory Guidelines for Managing Risks Associated with Acquisition, Development, and Construction Lending,* Financial Institution Letter (FIL)-110-98, dated October 8, 1998.

[15] *Insights From the FDIC's Credit and Consumer Products/Services Survey*, FDIC Supervisory Insights, Winter 2010.

[16] Section 337.12 of the FDIC's Rules and Regulations, which implements section 10(d) of the FDI Act, requires annual full-scope, on-site examinations of every state nonmember bank at least once every 12-month period and allows for 18-month intervals for certain small institutions (with total assets of less than $500 million) if certain conditions are satisfied.

[17] If there was no examination report in 2007, we used a 2006 report.

[18] *Banking Regulation: Enhanced Guidance on Commercial Real Estate Risks Needed*, GAO-11-489, May 2011.

In: Commercial Real Estate Lending
Editors: O. R. Sims and F. B. Fields
ISBN: 978-1-62618-617-0

Chapter 2

BANKING REGULATION: ENHANCED GUIDANCE ON COMMERCIAL REAL ESTATE RISKS NEEDED*

United States Government Accountability Office

WHY GAO DID THIS STUDY

Since the onset of the financial crisis in 2008, commercial real estate (CRE) loan delinquencies have more than doubled. The federal banking regulators have issued statements and guidance encouraging banks to continue lending to creditworthy borrowers and explaining how banks can work with troubled borrowers. However, some banks have stated that examiners' treatment of CRE loans has hampered their ability to lend.

This report examines, among other issues, (1) how the Federal Deposit Insurance Corporation (FDIC), Board of Governors of the Federal Reserve System (Federal Reserve), and the Office of the Comptroller of the Currency (OCC) responded to trends in CRE markets and the controls they have for helping ensure consistent application of guidance and (2) the relationships between bank supervision practices and lending. GAO reviewed agency guidance, examination review procedures, reports of examination, and relevant

* This is an edited, reformatted and augmented version of the Highlights of GAO-11-489, a report to the Ranking Member, Committee on Financial Services, House of Representatives, dated May 2011.

literature and interviewed agency officials, examiners, bank officials, and academics.

What GAO Recommends

Federal banking regulators should enhance or supplement the 2006 CRE concentration guidance and take steps to better ensure that such guidance is consistently applied. The Federal Reserve and OCC agreed with the recommendations. FDIC said that it had implemented strategies to supplement the 2006 guidance.

What GAO Found

Aware of the potential risks of growing CRE concentrations at community banks, federal banking regulators issued guidance on loan concentrations and risk management in 2006 and augmented it with guidance and statements on meeting credit needs and conducting CRE loan workouts from 2008 to 2010.

The regulators also conducted training on CRE treatment for examiners and internal reviews to help ensure compliance with CRE guidance. Nevertheless, a number of banks reported that examiners have been applying guidance more stringently since the financial crisis and believe that they have been too harsh in treatment of CRE loans.

Regulators have incorporated lessons learned from the crisis into their supervision approach, which may help explain banks' experiences of increased scrutiny. GAO found that examiners generally provided support for exam findings on loan workouts, but identified some inconsistencies in applying the 2006 CRE concentration guidance— which is similar to what some of the regulators uncovered in their internal reviews. Moreover, regulatory officials had varying views on the adequacy of the 2006 guidance, and some examiners and bankers noted that the guidance lacked clarity on how to comply with it. As a result, examiners and bankers may not have a common understanding about CRE concentration risks.

Although many factors influence banks' lending decisions, research shows that the capital banks hold is a key factor. Capital provides an important cushion against losses, but if a bank needs to increase it, the cost of raising capital can raise the cost of providing loans.

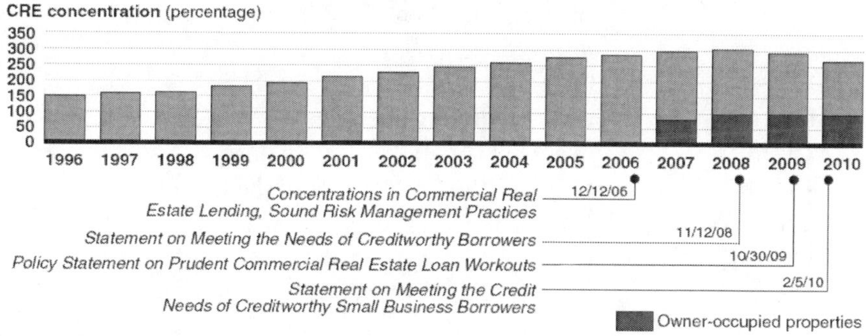

Source: GAO analysis of data from FDIC and regulatory guidance.

Average CRE Concentration among Community Banks and Regulatory Guidance.

High CRE concentrations also can limit a bank's ability to lend because the bank may need to raise capital to mitigate the concentration risk during a downturn. Economic research on the effect of regulators' examination practices on banks' lending decisions is limited, but shows that examiners' increased scrutiny during credit downturns can have a small impact on overall lending. Although isolating these impacts is difficult, the recent severe cycle of credit upswings followed by the downturn provides a useful reminder of the balance needed in bank supervision to help ensure the banking system can support economic recovery.

ABBREVIATIONS

ABA	American Bankers Association
ADC	acquisition, development, and construction
ALLL	allowance for loan and lease loss
CAMELS	Capital adequacy, Asset quality, Management, Earnings, Liquidity, and Sensitivity
CLD	construction and land development
CMBS	commercial mortgage-backed securities
CRE	commercial real estate
EIC	examiner-in-charge
FASB	Financial Accounting Standards Board
FDIC	Federal Deposit Insurance Corporation
Federal Reserve	Board of Governors of the Federal Reserve System
FFIEC	Federal Financial Institutions Examination Council

ICBA	Independent Community Bankers of America
IG	inspector general
MLR	material loss reviews
MRA	matter requiring attention
NCUA	National Credit Union Administration
OCC	Office of the Comptroller of the Currency
OTS	Office of Thrift Supervision
ROE	report of examination
TDR	troubled debt restructuring

May 19, 2011

The Honorable Barney Frank
Ranking Member
Committee on Financial Services
House of Representatives

Dear Mr. Frank:

The financial crisis, and the economic downturn that followed it, largely arose out of problems related to the residential mortgage sector, but the commercial real estate (CRE) market also has experienced significant setbacks, that in turn, have affected community banks.[1] More than a third of community bank lending is tied to CRE, and delinquencies for such loans have more than doubled since 2008. While segments of the CRE market have shown some improvement, problems in CRE lending are expected to continue, and refinancing such loans could present further challenges to the market in coming years. Banks are addressing these problems in many ways, including modifying borrowers' loan terms so that they can continue to make payments, increasing bank capital and reserves as protection against future losses, and, in some cases, reducing lending.[2] However, reduced lending to creditworthy borrowers can exacerbate credit tightening and inhibit economic recovery.

The federal banking regulators have been monitoring the increasing CRE concentrations for a number of years and have responded to the current CRE downturn and its impact on the banks they supervise. The regulators have issued interagency statements and guidance—most recently from 2006 through 2010—on managing the risks of CRE concentrations, encouraging banks to continue lending to creditworthy borrowers, clarifying to banks how examiners will review loans secured by CRE, and explaining how banks can work with troubled borrowers.[3] Regulators have also noted concerns they have about the risk-management systems of banks with high CRE concentrations and have "classified" more loans (that is, identified loans that pose a risk of loss to banks).[4] In doing so, examiners have been criticized by some in the banking industry for being too harsh in their treatment of CRE loans in banks' portfolios, and some argue that this has hampered lending more broadly in communities across the country.

In light of these questions about examiners' treatment of CRE loans, you asked us to review whether examiners' practices related to CRE were consistent with recent regulatory statements and guidance; whether regulatory views on regulators' bank ratings, capital, and liquidity have changed; and what the potential impact of regulatory practices might be on lending by community banks. This report examines (1) the condition of the CRE market and the implications for community banks; (2) how three federal banking regulators—the Federal Deposit Insurance Corporation (FDIC), Board of Governors of the Federal Reserve System (Federal Reserve), and the Office of the Comptroller of the Currency (OCC)— responded to trends in CRE markets through their supervision of community banks and what controls they have to help ensure consistent application of policy guidance; and (3) what is known about the relationships between bank supervision practices and lending.

To address our objectives related to the condition of the CRE market and its implications for community banks, we analyzed data from 1996 through 2010 (when available) from Moody's/REAL Commercial Property Price Index for CRE values and call report data for CRE loan concentrations and performance.[5] We reviewed CRE-related reports from the Congressional Oversight Panel, Congressional Research Service, FDIC, Federal Reserve, and academic journals, and conducted interviews with bank examiners, regulatory officials, and community bankers. We also examined material loss reviews (MLR) conducted by the inspectors general (IG) of the bank regulators and previous GAO products. To understand how FDIC, the Federal Reserve, and OCC have responded to the CRE downturn, we collected and analyzed regulatory guidance related to CRE loan treatment and interagency statements on lending, and also assessed regulatory efforts to address CRE-related concerns.[6] As part of this work, we observed training provided by the Federal Financial Institutions Examination Council (FFIEC) to examiners related to CRE guidance and loan classifications.[7]

To understand bank officials' concerns about examiners' treatment of CRE loans, we spoke with officials from 43 community banks and analyzed 55 bank reports of examination (ROE). For our bank official interviews, we contacted 62 banks and spoke with all 21 that responded to us based on a nonprobability sample of banks in California, Georgia, Massachusetts, and Texas. We chose those states because banks in the first two states have had a relatively greater share of CRE-related nonperforming loans (as measured by the percentage of CRE loans past due or on nonaccrual) and banks in the last two a relatively smaller share.[8] From these states, we selected banks that had a federal bank regulator examination after October 2009; elevated concentrations in CRE; or elevated concentrations in acquisition, development, and construction (ADC) loans.[9] This sampling approach also was used to select the 55 ROEs for analysis. Our sample is not designed to be generalizable to all banks, but instead provides information on a range of banks working under different supervisors, having different conditions, and operating in different economic environments. For our bank official interviews, we supplemented the sample by interviewing officials from 22 additional banks that testified before Congress on the issue of CRE, were identified through bank associations, or requested an interview after learning about our work.

To understand examiners' practices and views on certain regulatory measures, especially on the CRE loan workout guidance, we spoke with regulatory staff at district, regional, and field offices in California, Colorado, Georgia, Massachusetts, and Texas, and in headquarters at Washington, D.C. We spoke with more than 230 field staff in various roles (either directly involved in drafting and reviewing ROEs or participating in oversight of the review process)—both in group settings and individually. While not representative of the population of examiners and regulatory staff, our interviews with examiners and other regulatory staff provide a broad range of views. To understand the controls the regulators have in place to help ensure consistent application of policy guidance, we collected, compared, and analyzed examination review reports and quality assurance processes for the three regulators, and also interviewed officials. To understand what is known about the relationships between regulators' supervision practices, lending, and CRE values, we conducted a literature review dating to 1991 and focusing on comprehensive, empirical, published research that reviewed such topics and also interviewed academics, regulatory officials, and bank officials.

We conducted this performance audit from May 2010 through May 2011 in accordance with generally accepted government auditing standards. Those standards require that we plan and perform the audit to obtain sufficient, appropriate evidence to provide a reasonable basis for our findings and conclusions based on our audit objectives. We believe that the evidence obtained provides a reasonable basis for our findings and conclusions based on our audit objectives.[10]

Background

As of December 31, 2010, there were 6,364 community banks (commercial banks with total assets of $1 billion or less). This represents about 92 percent of all commercial banks, although only about 10 percent of commercial bank assets nationwide. Banks in the United States are supervised by one of the following three federal regulators:

- FDIC supervises all FDIC-insured state-chartered banks that are not members of the Federal Reserve System.
- The Federal Reserve supervises commercial banks that are state-chartered and members of the Federal Reserve System.
- OCC supervises federally chartered national banks.

Table 1 summarizes the regulators' oversight responsibilities for community banks.

Table 1. Regulatory Overview Information for FDIC, the Federal Reserve, and OCC (as of December 31, 2010)

Dollars in millions					
Regulator	Bank type supervised	Number of banks supervised	Number of community banks (less than $1 billion total assets) supervised	Total assets under supervision	Total assets under supervision at banks with less than $1 billion in total assets
Federal Reserve	State-chartered member banks of Federal Reserve System	829	729	$1,697.0	$167.2
FDIC	State nonmember banks; savings institutions	4,715	4,414	2,259.1	865.4
OCC	Federally chartered national banks	1,383	1,221	8,432.3	267.7
Total		**6,927**	**6,364**	**$12,388.4**	**$1,300.3**

Source: GAO analysis of FDIC call report data.

The purpose of federal banking supervision is to help ensure that banks throughout the financial system are operating in a safe and sound manner, and are complying with banking laws and regulations in the provision of financial services. As we have identified in previous work, financial regulation more broadly has sought to achieve four goals: to (1) ensure adequate consumer protections, (2) ensure the integrity and fairness of markets, (3) monitor the safety and soundness of institutions, and (4) act to ensure the stability of the overall financial system.[11] Federal banking regulators use a number of tools to achieve these goals.

- **Capital requirements:** Regulators require banks to maintain certain minimum capital requirements to help ensure the safety and soundness of the banking system, and generally expect banks to hold capital above these minimums—commensurate with their risks. Capital provides an important cushion against losses for banks, and represents the amount of money that can cover losses the bank may face related to nonpayment of loans and other losses on assets. Capital can be measured as total capital or tier 1 capital.[12] Regulators oversee the capital adequacy of their regulated institutions through ongoing monitoring, including on-site examinations and off-site tools. When regulators require banks to hold capital above regulatory minimums, these requirements may result from an enforcement action through an agreement between the regulator and the bank. However, requiring banks to hold more capital may reduce the availability of bank credit and reduce returns on equity to shareholders.
- **Examinations and ratings:** Federal banking laws and regulatory guidance require on-site examinations, which serve to evaluate a bank's overall risk exposure and its ability to identify and manage those risks— especially as they affect a bank's financial health. At each full-scope examination, examiners review the bank's risk exposure on a number of components using what is known as the CAMELS rating system (Capital adequacy, Asset quality, Management, Earnings, Liquidity, and Sensitivity to market risk). Evaluations of CAMELS components consider the institution's size and sophistication, the nature and complexity of its activities, and its risk profile. In examinations, a bank is rated for each of the CAMELS components and given a composite rating, which generally bears a close relationship to the component ratings. However, the composite is not an average of the component ratings. The component rating and

the composite ratings are scored on a scale of 1 (best) to 5 (worst). Regulatory actions typically correspond to the composite CAMELS ratings, with the actions generally increasing in severity as the ratings become worse. Table 2 describes the definitions of the composite scores under the Uniform Financial Institutions Rating System.[13]

Table 2. CAMELS Composite Score Definitions

Composite score	Definition
1	Banks in this group are sound in every respect and generally have components rated 1 or 2. These banks are the most capable of withstanding changing business conditions. These banks exhibit the strongest performance and risk-management practices relative to the bank's size, complexity, and risk profile and give no cause for regulatory concern.
2	Banks in this group are fundamentally sound and generally should not have component ratings worse than 3. Only moderate weaknesses are present and are within the bank's management capabilities to correct. Risk-management practices are satisfactory and there are no material regulatory concerns.
3	Banks in this group exhibit some degree of regulatory concern in one or more of the component areas. These banks exhibit a combination of weaknesses that may range from weak to moderate and management may lack the ability or willingness to effectively address these weaknesses. These banks are generally less capable of withstanding business fluctuations than 1 or 2 rated banks. Risk-management practices may be less than satisfactory but failure appears unlikely.
4	Banks in this group generally exhibit unsafe and unsound practices or conditions. There are serious financial or managerial deficiencies that may range from severe to critically deficient. Banks in this group are generally not capable of withstanding business fluctuations. Risk-management practices generally are unacceptable relative to the institution's size, complexity, and risk profile. Failure is a distinct possibility if problems are not addressed and resolved.
5	Banks in this group exhibit extremely unsafe and unsound practices or conditions; exhibit critically deficient performance; often contain inadequate risk-management practices relative to the bank's size, complexity, and risk profile; and are the greatest regulatory concern.

Source: Federal Reserve.

- **Loan classifications:** In examinations, examiners review a sample of banks' internal ratings of loans to determine the adequacy of credit risk administration and identify loans that show undue risk and may be uncollectible. As part of this review, examiners determine which loans are considered "pass," with no concerns noted, as well as those that are special mentioned or "classified"—that is, subject to criticism because they are not performing or may not perform in the future. There are three classification categories used by the federal banking regulators: substandard, doubtful, and loss (see table 3). These loan classifications, and the internal ratings that banks produce for all of their loans, are incorporated into how each bank calculates its allowance for loan and lease loss (ALLL), which is an estimate made according to accounting guidance of incurred losses on loans and leases.[14] Therefore, if additional loans are classified substandard or doubtful, this information is included in a bank's updated ALLL estimates. If loans are classified loss, they are charged off the bank's balance sheet.[15]

The end result of an on-site examination is an ROE that includes the CAMELS ratings and other findings on the bank's condition, which is provided to the bank's management and board of directors.

Table 3. Regulatory Loan Classification System

Classification	Definition
Substandard	Loans that are inadequately protected by the current sound worth and paying capacity of the obligor or of the collateral pledged, if any. Loans so classified must have a well-defined weakness or weaknesses that jeopardize the liquidation of the debt. They are characterized by the distinct possibility that the bank will sustain some loss if the deficiencies are not corrected.
Doubtful	Loans that have all the weaknesses inherent in those classified substandard with the added characteristic that the weaknesses make collection or liquidation in full, on the basis of currently known facts, conditions, and values, highly questionable and improbable.
Loss	Loans that are considered uncollectible and of such little value that their continuance as bankable assets is not warranted. This classification does not mean that the loan has absolutely no recovery or salvage value but rather it is not practical or desirable to defer writing off this basically worthless asset even though partial recovery may be effected in the future.

Source: Federal Reserve.

CRE Property Types and Associated Risks

CRE encompasses many different property types that present different risks. Table 4 describes the key CRE property types.

Regulators define CRE loans to include construction loans, loans to finance CRE that are not secured by CRE, loans secured by multifamily property, and loans secured by nonfarm, nonresidential property in which the primary source of repayment derives from the rental income associated with the property or the proceeds of the sale, refinancing, or permanent financing of the property. CRE loans in which the primary source of repayment is not the property itself are called owner-occupied loans and can include loans to businesses for working capital purposes that use real estate as collateral.[16] For example, a line of credit for a business's operating expenses might be secured in part by commercial property, such as an office.

Owner-occupied properties generally are considered to carry less risk than non-owner-occupied properties because regulators consider them to be less sensitive to the condition of the CRE market. In ADC loans, also called construction and land development (CLD) loans, generally are considered to be the riskiest class of CRE, due to their long development times and because they can include properties (such as housing developments or retail space in a shopping mall) that are built before having firm commitments from buyers or lessees. In addition, by the time the construction phase is completed, market demand may have fallen, putting downward pressure on sales prices or rents—making this type of loan more volatile. In recent years, this type of loan also has tended to have a much higher loss volatility than loans secured by properties such as multifamily housing and other nonfarm, nonresidential commercial properties.

Banks report on four broad categories of CRE in their quarterly call reports:

- CLD: loans secured by real estate to finance land development and construction. This includes new construction, as well as additions and alterations on existing properties.
- Multifamily: loans for residential properties with five or more dwelling units, such as apartment buildings.
- Nonfarm nonresidential: loans secured by real estate for business and industrial properties, as well as properties such as hotels, churches, hospitals, schools, and charitable organizations. This category includes offices, retail, and warehouse space.
- Loans to finance CRE, construction, and land development (not secured by CRE).

Interagency guidance issued in 2006 on concentrations in CRE and sound risk-management practices define CRE loans within these categories to include those in which repayment is dependent on the cash flow generated from the real estate itself. When evaluating concentrations in CRE, examiners are instructed not to include owner-occupied properties in which the income or value of the property is not the primary source of repayment.

Deterioration of the CRE Market Negatively Affected Community Banks, Which Could Impact Small Business Lending

The CRE Market Has Experienced a Significant Downturn

CRE as an asset class—and especially properties in the ADC category—is prone to volatility and cyclical behavior, as illustrated in the current CRE market downturn. This volatility and cyclical behavior is attributed to characteristics such as information-gathering difficulties, infrequent transactions, high transaction costs, rigid and constrained supply, long construction times, and a two-fold reliance on external finance (shorter-term to cover construction, and longer-term for the occupancy period).[17] Additionally, CRE is by nature diverse and localized. For example, shopping centers are one type of CRE, but even within this category properties can have significant differences depending on design, types of tenants, and other factors that can affect their value. Because of these factors, the supply of CRE in the marketplace is slow to respond to an increase in demand, which drives prices up when investor optimism rises. Conversely, the marketplace is slow to respond when the market supply of CRE catches up and new construction projects are delivered, resulting in oversupply and declining property values. According to regulatory officials, the weakness in the ADC sector during this crisis was primarily due to residential housing construction, and that weakness affected the performance of other areas of CRE (for example, failed residential housing developments will affect the ability of nearby strip malls to attract and generate rental income from tenants).

The recent downturn in the CRE markets can be seen in the market values for commercial property and the condition of the commercial mortgage-backed securities (CMBS) market. [18] Market values for all major commercial property types have declined significantly. As of December 2010, overall CRE market values were down more than 42 percent from their peak in 2007. This decline followed a rapid appreciation in CRE asset values during which CRE values increased by more than 85 percent from 2002 to the market's peak in October 2007 (see figure 1).

Overall deterioration in CRE markets can be found in the condition of the CMBS market as well. By January 2011, the delinquency rate on loans included in CMBS was at a record high, above 9 percent. As we have reported, overall CMBS issuance slowed severely since the CRE downturn started. After peaking in 2007, the CMBS market came to a complete halt by the end of 2008.[19]

Table 4. Key CRE Property Types

Property types	Definition
Retail	Malls, major retailers, strip malls and small, local retail businesses. These properties depend on the cash flow of the resident businesses and are closely tied to consumer demand and the overall economy.
Hotel/tourist	All types of hotel and motel properties. These properties' cash flows depend on levels of occupancy and the daily rate charged. In addition to being tied to trends in tourism and the overall economy, the hotel sector also is vulnerable to fluctuations in local economies and conditions.
Office buildings	Includes diverse properties in which office occupancy is the dominant use. Office properties may be more stable due to their longer lease cycles than other CRE property types.
Industrial	Warehouses, manufacturing plants, light industrial plants, laboratories, and research properties.
Multifamily housing and apartments	Buildings with multiple dwelling units for rent. These properties, unlike most residential properties, are income generating and use the commercial mortgage market for financing.
Homebuilders	The development of residential properties and loans to businesses that develop residential properties.

Source: Congressional Oversight Panel (COP).

Note: This information is from the Congressional Oversight Panel's February 10, 2010, report *Commercial Real Estate Losses and the Risk to Financial Stability*.

Although CRE market price deterioration appears to have leveled off recently, vacancies at many properties remain high and signs of a market recovery have been uneven in different areas of the country. High-value properties in markets such as New York, Washington, San Francisco, and Boston have performed well more recently.[20] But low rental rates and high vacancies indicate that demand for office, retail, multifamily housing, and warehouse space remains relatively weak.[21]

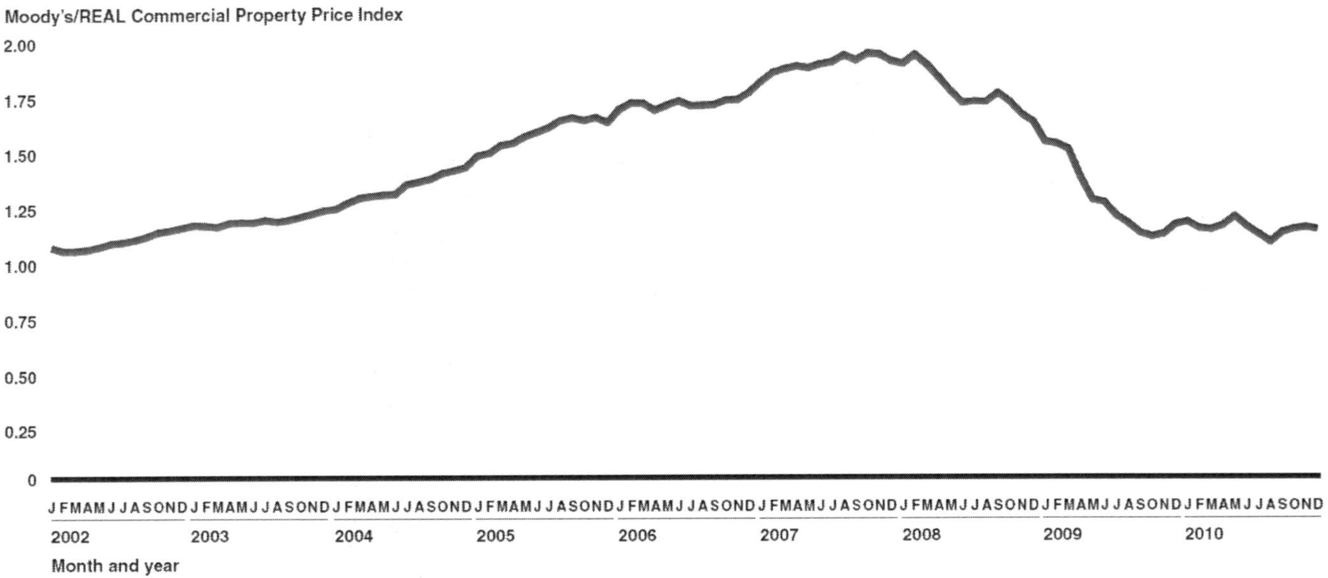

Source: Moody's/REAL Commercial Property Price Index.

Figure 1. Trends in Commercial Property Price Index (from 2002 through 2010).

Furthermore, although CRE markets nationally have experienced a downturn, some regions have experienced more distress than others. For example, the CRE markets in the South, Midwest, and West have experienced greater stress and deterioration than the East.[22] These areas that have experienced greater CRE market stress also have experienced more bank failures, according to FDIC data.

The Decline of the CRE Market Has Adversely Affected Community Banks

Community banks increasingly have moved toward providing CRE loans more than other kinds of loan products, in part because of competitive pressures. During the last decade, large banks and other financial institutions increased their market share for consumer loans, credit cards, and residential mortgages. As a result, community banks shifted their focus to CRE lending. Some market observers argue that community banks' focus on CRE lending, and, therefore, the long-term trend of increased CRE concentrations, came about because community banks generally know their local CRE markets better than larger banks and are well-positioned to gather location-specific information for CRE properties.

The increased exposure of community banks to CRE loans has been pronounced over the last 10–15 years. While CRE collateral backed about 30 percent of total loans and leases at community banks in 2000, a decade later that rate increased to more than 43 percent. Concentrations have been less pronounced at larger banks, which tend to rely less heavily on CRE lending. Since 2000, CRE as a percent of total loans and leases has ranged from about 15 percent to about 21 percent at commercial banks with more than $1 billion in total assets.

Community banks also have come to hold large concentrations of CRE loans in comparison to their total capital. The average CRE concentration at community banks as a percentage of total risk-based capital increased from about 168 percent in 1996–2000 to about 289 percent in 2005–2010 (see figure 2). Increased exposure to CRE has made community banks vulnerable to the decline of this market. According to FDIC, nearly 30 percent of community banks have concentrations of CRE to total capital above 300 percent, the concentration threshold established in the 2006 interagency guidance on CRE, above which regulators review banks' risk-management controls more closely.

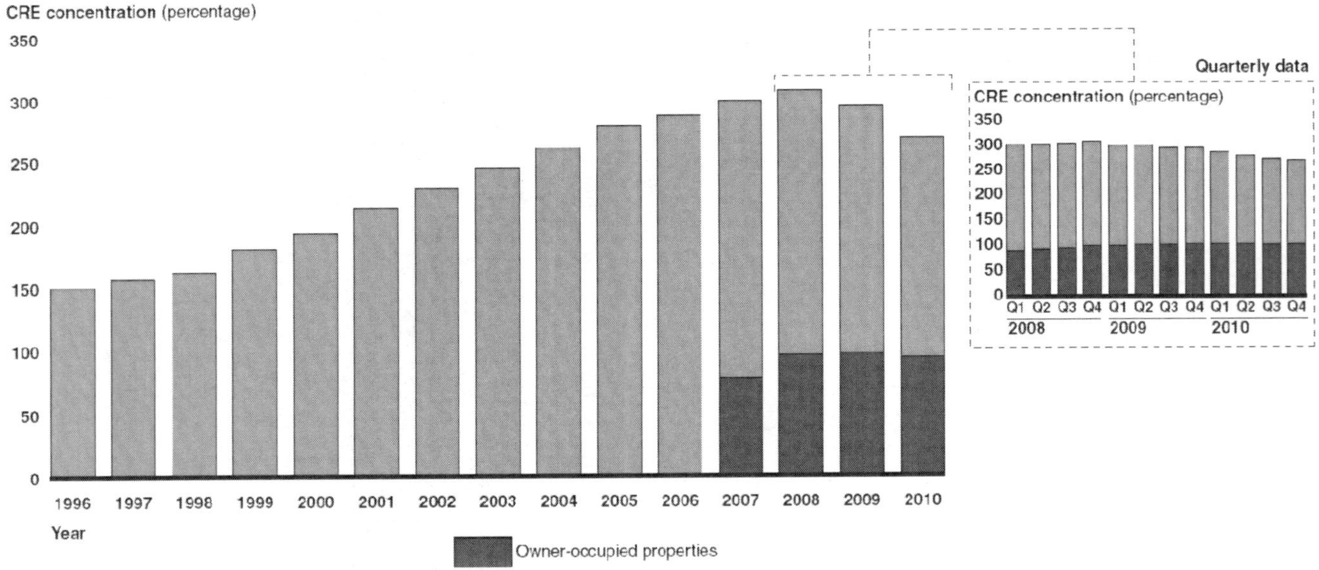

Source: GAO analysis of data from FDIC.

Note: The CRE concentrations represented in this graphic include loans secured by owner-occupied CRE. Call report data did not begin specifying whether CRE was owner-occupied until 2007.

Figure 2. Average CRE Concentrations at Community Banks (from 1996 through 2010).

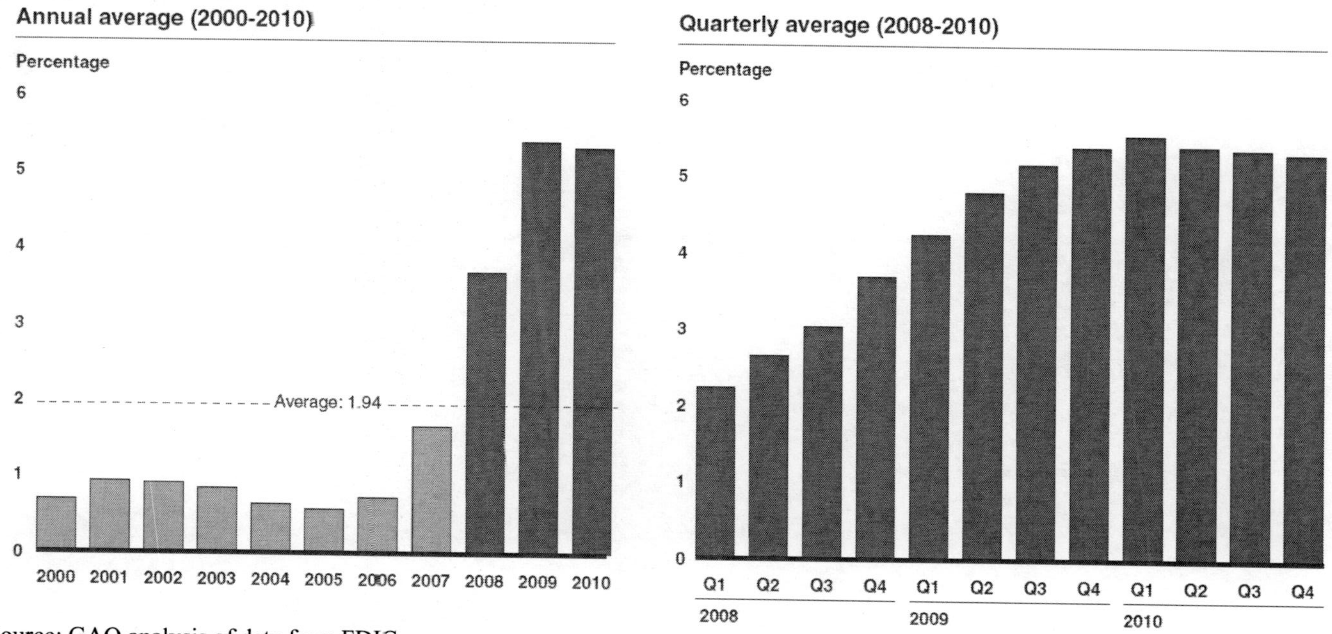

Source: GAO analysis of data from FDIC.

Figure 3. Percent of Noncurrent Loans Secured by CRE at Community Banks (from 2000 through 2010).

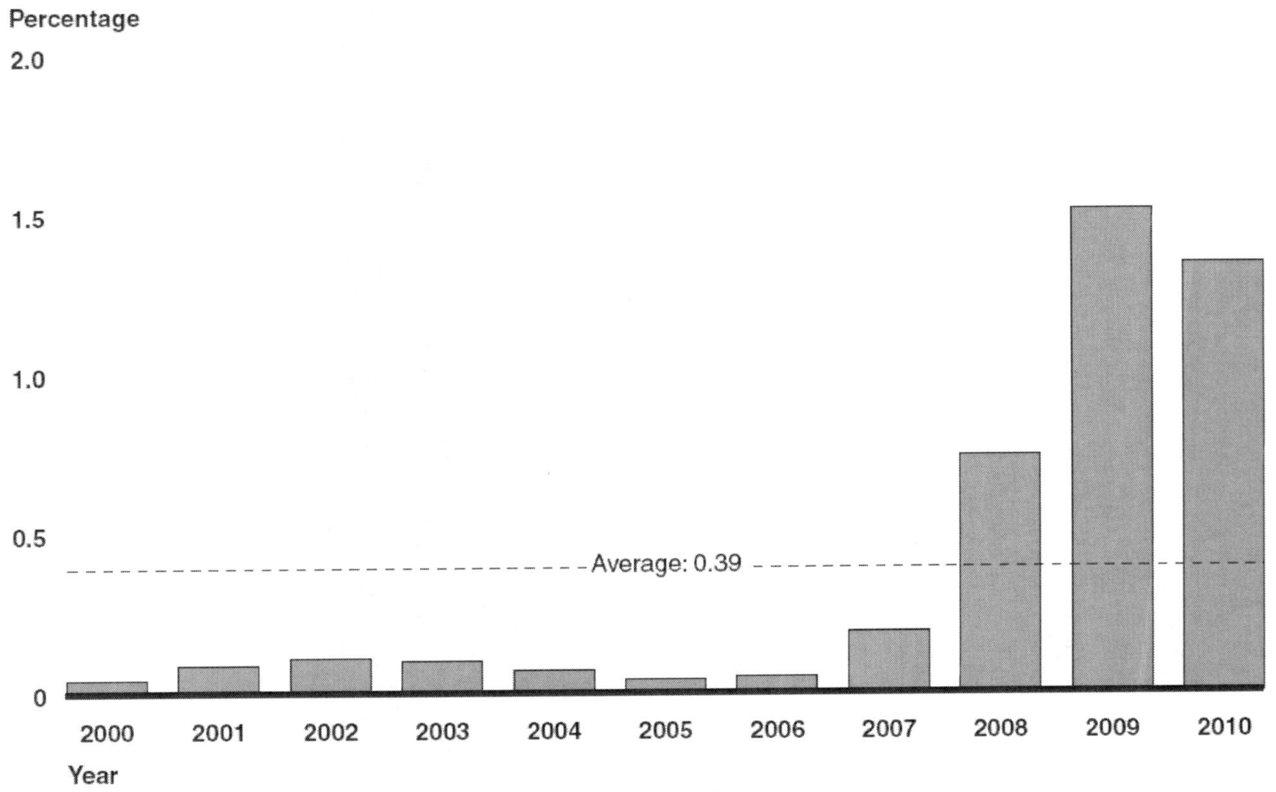

Source: GAO analysis of data from FDIC.

Figure 4. Average Charge-off Rate for Loans Secured by CRE at Community Banks (from 2000 through 2010).

This means that nearly a third of community banks are exposing three times their total capital to risks related to their CRE loans.

As noted by a Bank for International Settlements report on bank lending and commercial property cycles, declining property prices increase the proportion of nonperforming loans, lead to a deterioration in banks' balance sheets, and weaken banks' capital bases.[23]

In particular, the decline in CRE values has contributed to more noncurrent CRE loans, charge-offs, and bank failures.

- **Noncurrent CRE loans have increased.** From the first quarter of 2008 through the fourth quarter of 2010, the percent of CRE loans at community banks that were noncurrent increased from 2.2 to 5.3 percent, well above the average rate of 0.9 percent from 2000 through 2007. The average from 2000 through 2010 is 1.94 percent. However, the data show that the volume of noncurrent CRE loans has begun to level off (see figure 3).
- **CRE loan charge-offs increased.** From the end of 2007 through the end of 2010, the percent of CRE loans that had to be charged off at community banks rose from 0.19 to 1.34 percent. From 2000 through 2007, the average charge off rate of CRE loans at community banks was 0.09 percent, and from 2000 through 2010 it was 0.39 percent (see figure 4). Charge-offs and expected losses that may arise from increases in noncurrent CRE loans have put stress on banks' capital and ALLL.
- **Increased bank failures linked to high CRE and ADC concentrations.** Many bank failures are associated with high CRE and ADC concentrations. In 2009 and 2010, 102 of 106 of the MLRs issued by the IGs of the banking regulators cited high CRE concentrations, and 92 of 106 specifically cited ADC loans in particular as a contributing factor in bank failures. In the 106 MLRs, 76 of the banks reviewed were community banks.[24] For example, the MLR for one failed bank—which contains findings similar to many other MLRs we reviewed—states that the rapid growth of its CRE portfolio "increased the institution's exposure to a sustained downturn in the real estate market and reduced its ability to absorb losses due to unforeseen events."

Depressed CRE Markets Could Reduce Small Business Lending

CRE market value declines could reduce overall small business lending by community banks. As we previously reported, community banks tend to have a larger portion of small-business related loans compared with larger banks.[25] Because CRE can be used as collateral for small business loans, diminished CRE values also can negatively affect credit availability to small businesses. Specifically, when the value of collateral declines, the amount of financing a bank is willing to lend against that collateral typically declines as well. Conversely, increases in collateral values lower the premium on external financing—improving credit availability for borrowers, boosting demand for real estate assets, and driving up prices. Therefore, falling property prices can generate a cycle of declining CRE values because they can accompany reduced credit. A report by the Bank for International Settlements notes that falling CRE prices decrease the value of collateral held by banks and, therefore, can give rise to significant losses by these banks and ultimately contract the supply of credit.[26]

The problem of CRE loan refinancing may exacerbate the negative CRE trends and limit lending to small businesses. CRE loans usually are written for 3–10 years, with a 20–30 year amortization schedule and a balloon payment at the end. Instead of making the large balloon payment, the borrower typically will sell the property or refinance the loan at the end of the term. Small businesses that are looking to refinance a loan against a property that has lost a significant amount of market value may have to put up more equity. Alternatively, such borrowers might default on the loan, or the bank could work with the borrower to restructure the loan and avoid default. Trepp LLC, a commercial mortgage analysis firm, estimates that about $1.7 trillion in CRE mortgages will mature between 2011 and 2015, with about half of that held at banks. Moreover, Trepp estimates that approximately 60 percent of CRE debt maturing in 2011 is "underwater"—meaning the value of the loan exceeds the value of the underlying collateral. Due to price declines and stricter bank underwriting standards compared to when these loans were originated, those mortgages will be difficult to refinance.

Results from the Federal Reserve's Senior Loan Officer Opinion Survey have suggested that new CRE borrowers have faced tighter credit conditions, due to banks tightening their underwriting standards in response to the downturn. The January 2011 survey found that 10.6 percent of respondents reported easing credit standards over the previous 3 months, compared to 10.5 percent who reported tightening them. However, this is a positive development from past results that showed severe tightening.[27] The trend of tighter credit standards suggests that borrowers who previously were considered creditworthy might not meet banks' higher standards.

While Regulators Have Taken Steps to Address CRE Concentrations and Bank Concerns, Challenges Remain in Consistently Applying Guidance

The regulators have been aware for some time of the risk-management challenges related to growing CRE concentrations at community banks and have taken steps to address these challenges. The regulators, for example, issued guidance to banks on managing CRE concentration risks, conducted training on CRE treatment, and conducted internal reviews to better ensure examiner compliance with CRE guidance. Even with the training and reviews, a number of bank officials we interviewed stated that regulators have applied guidance rigidly since the financial crisis and have been too harsh in classifying loans and improperly applying the 2006 CRE guidance, among other issues. Regulators have been incorporating lessons from the financial crisis in their supervisory practices, which in part may explain bank officials' experience of increased stringency in supervision. Based on our review of a nonprobability sample of 55 bank examinations, examiners' findings were consistent with CRE loan workout guidance, although in some instances examiners did not clearly support requirements for reduced CRE concentrations and did not calculate CRE concentrations according to concentration and risk-management guidance. Additionally, senior regulatory officials and examiners have differing views on the adequacy of the 2006 guidance, which may affect how consistently the guidance is applied.

Federal Banking Regulators Addressed CRE Issues Before and After the Financial Crisis by Issuing Guidance on CRE Concentrations and Loan Workouts

The regulators began to address CRE concerns before the financial crisis. Beginning in the early 2000s, the agencies reviewed CRE concentrations and risk-management systems across banks. For example, an OCC review found potential for improvement in banks' risk-management processes for CRE concentrations, including the sufficiency of stress testing. The regulators issued draft guidance in January 2006 on CRE concentrations and risk management, based in part on the trends they had observed in CRE concentrations and risks.[28] The draft guidance elicited considerable feedback from bank representatives, many of whom stated it would curtail their CRE lending, impose arbitrary limits on CRE concentrations, and require additional capital without explicitly stating how much would be required. The regulators revised the guidance based on the feedback received. Issued in final form in December 2006, the interagency guidance provides levels of CRE concentrations that will result in additional regulatory attention on risk-management systems: (1) 300 percent of CRE loans to total capital, (2) increases of 50 percent or more in CRE loans during the prior 36 months, and (3) 100 percent of CLD (or ADC) loans to total capital. In determining the concentration ratio, owner-occupied CRE is removed.[29] The guidance also states that the concentration numbers are not limits, but rather indicate when banks will receive closer scrutiny of risk-management systems and capital adequacy. Such thresholds are not intended to be a "safe harbor"—that is, banks with lower concentrations may still receive scrutiny of their CRE loans in examinations—and banks that exhibit other risk factors can receive criticisms on their CRE concentrations.[30]

In October 2009, after the start of the financial crisis and the widespread deterioration in CRE loan performance, regulators issued interagency guidance on CRE loan workouts.[31] According to the regulators, the guidance was issued to (1) help ensure consistent CRE loan and workout treatment among the regulators, (2) update and re-assert previous guidance, (3) inform banks of examiner expectations, and (4) ensure that supervisory practices do not inadvertently curtail the availability of credit to sound borrowers. Officials told us that the guidance was not intended as forbearance, but to encourage prudent loan workouts. While the 2009 guidance was similar to that issued in 1991 and 1993, regulatory officials noted that it includes updates for changes in accounting (for example, related to ALLL), information on risk management for CRE loan workouts, and numerous examples to assist banks and examiners in interpreting the guidance. The examples provide scenarios for different CRE loan classification outcomes and whether loans should be considered troubled debt restructurings (TDR), among other issues.[32] Bankers with whom we spoke stated that the examples were helpful in understanding how to apply the guidance. Examiners told us that the examples have helped to resolve differences of opinion with bankers on how to treat certain CRE-related loans. In addition to the 2009 CRE loan workout guidance, the regulators issued statements on lending to creditworthy borrowers and creditworthy small business borrowers to encourage prudent lending among banks and balanced supervision among examiners.

Regulators Rely on a Variety of Processes to Help Ensure Examinations of CRE Portfolios Are Consistent and Appropriate, and Some Processes Have Identified Inconsistencies

Federal banking regulators help ensure consistency among examinations, and appropriate application of guidance, primarily through the ROE review process—but also through training, internal reviews, quality assurance processes, and processes for obtaining input from banks. Such processes reflect federal internal control standards, which provide reasonable assurance that management directives are carried out. The federal government standards for internal control state that managers should have controls in place to compare actual performance to planned or expected results over time throughout the organization and analyze significant differences.[33] All of the regulators' processes were used in some form to implement CRE guidance and ensure consistent treatment of CRE loans. Some of the internal review processes have identified inconsistencies in the application of CRE guidance.

ROE Review Process

The regulators' examination drafting and review process is iterative, with multiple levels of internal review. According to regulatory staff, this design helps ensure consistent application of guidance and treatment of banks. Figure 5 illustrates the examination process of the federal banking regulators. The process and the staff involved vary slightly for each regulator and based on a bank's CAMELS rating.

For all examinations, a team of examiners will conduct on-site work, led by an examiner-in-charge (EIC), who drafts the ROE. Other staff and management also discuss findings with the examination team and review the examination report. The case manager in particular helps ensure consistency. Case managers review draft ROEs for consistency and adequate support of findings for a portfolio of banks.

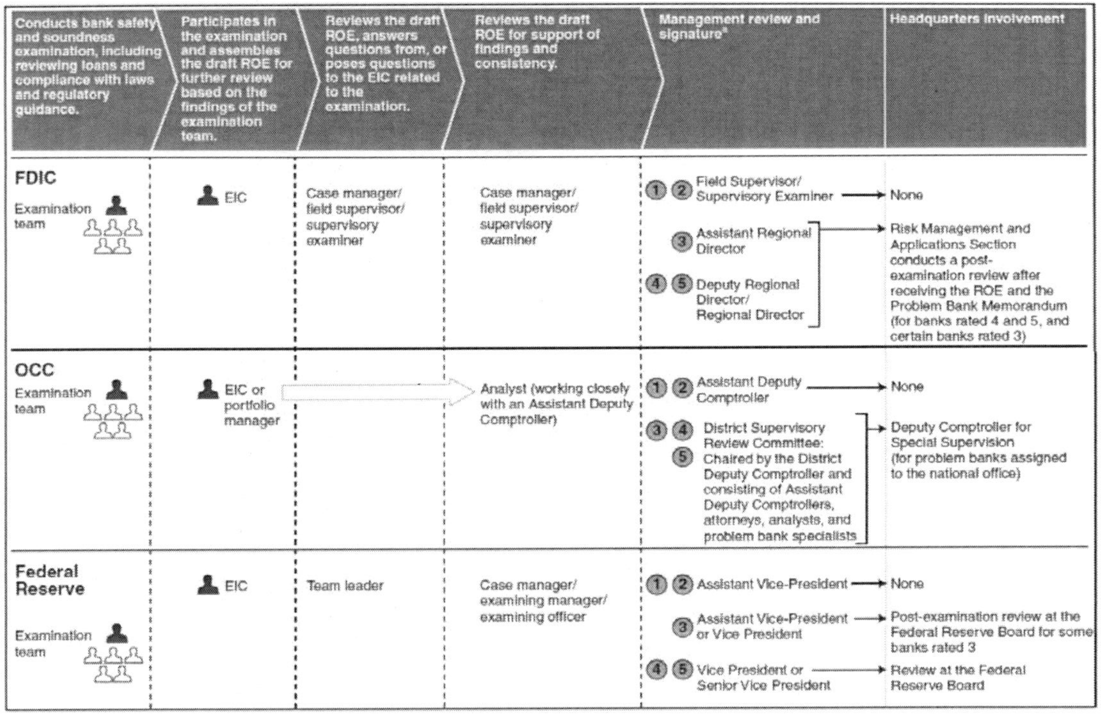

(#) CAMELS composite rating

Source: GAO.

[a] Signature authority may vary based on regional delegations of authority.

Figure 5. The Community Bank Examination Review Process at FDIC, the Federal Reserve, and OCC.

The analyst function at OCC serves a similar role: reviewing many ROEs, although not assigned to a specific portfolio of banks. While case managers and senior management generally do not review loan classification details, they review loan classification writeups in ROEs for accuracy and support for CAMELS ratings in a broad range of ROEs. According to Federal Reserve officials, case managers and senior management hold discussions with the examination teams as examination findings are being finalized, to ensure that they are appropriate. Therefore, these roles help ensure consistent application of guidance among various examiners. In certain instances, the regulators' headquarters offices in Washington, D.C., may participate to help ensure consistent implementation of policy guidance.

Training

Regulators also provide training on new guidance to help ensure consistent application. All the agencies offered multiple training opportunities or conference calls on the 2006 CRE concentration and the 2009 CRE loan workout guidance. For the 2009 CRE loan workout guidance, Federal Reserve and FDIC headquarters staff visited field offices, and all regulators hosted conference calls with examiners to better ensure that the field examiners were implementing it as intended. Some field offices also included these CRE topics in their own training and team meetings.[34]

Internal Audits and Quality Assurance Processes

Regulators also have internal reviews and quality assurance processes to help promote consistency, including consistent application of the CRE guidance. Regulators' internal reviews include comprehensive audits that recur periodically, and real-time and post-ROE quality processes.[35] Some of these reviews identified inconsistencies or other needed improvements related to examiner treatment of CRE loans. For example:

- For certain FDIC regions, reviews found that examiners could have better documented findings on CRE concentrations or could have provided earlier or harsher criticism of CRE concentrations, and the regional office could have better monitored CRE concentrations among the banks it supervised. According to an FDIC official, the regions already have addressed some of these findings.[36]
- Certain districts of the Federal Reserve System reviewed implementation of the 2006 CRE concentration guidance and found instances of inconsistency.[37] The reports concluded that the guidance

could have clarified expectations for how examiners should review banks' compliance with CRE-related risk-management practices and noted that a common, mandatory process for reviewing banks' compliance with the 2006 guidance would have resulted in better documentation and consistency. In particular, these reviews found that examination workpapers sometimes lacked sufficient documentation to determine if the examiner adequately assessed compliance with the guidance, particularly related to CRE portfolio-level stress testing. According to Federal Reserve officials, Washington staff also coordinated separate reviews related to implementation of the 2006 guidance, which resulted in internal clarifications of the appraisal review process, ALLL assessment guidance, examiner training sessions on the use of interest reserves and TDRs, and contributions to the 2009 loan workout guidance.

- According to a San Francisco Federal Reserve Bank official, the San Francisco Federal Reserve Bank implemented a "look back" process in June 2010 in which a senior official reviews the sufficiency of support for downgraded CRE loans for all issued ROEs—in response to criticism that examiners were being too harsh and curtailing credit. Of 11 CRE loan downgrades reviewed in the third and fourth quarter of 2010, this official stated that 2 should not have been downgraded.[38] Specifically, according to this official, the loans initially were considered collateral dependent, but after closer review the official determined that the borrowers had some capacity to repay, so the loans should have been classified but not yet charged off. In these two cases, the loan downgrades were reviewed and changed before the ROEs were finalized and were consistent with the bank's internal loan ratings. According to this official, the findings from this quality process will be used to improve the accuracy of CRE loan classification.
- Similarly, all OCC districts instituted a real-time review process in which experienced staff reviewed the accuracy of CRE loan classifications— before the ROE is finalized.[39] For example, OCC's central district in January 2009 reported that 95 percent of examiners' ratings decisions on CRE loans, and 99 percent of their accrual decisions, were determined to be accurate. Among those classifications that were corrected, 3 percent were downgraded and 2 percent were upgraded. Based on these findings, the district concluded that the vast majority of examiner loan classifications were accurate

but recommended more training to address the discrepancies. The western district's quality assurance process concluded that 4 percent of risk ratings were incorrect.[40]

Processes for Obtaining Bank Feedback

Regulators also use surveys to gather information on how to improve the examination process and understand the impact of policies on the banking industry.[41] For example, the regulators issued an interagency survey for examinations conducted between May 31 and July 9, 2010. According to an FDIC analysis of the resulting data, more than 97 percent of respondents stated that the 2009 CRE loan workout guidance has been helpful. In addition, nearly 88 percent of banks stated that no specific guidance was inhibiting them from working with troubled borrowers. Among the remaining 12 percent, just over three-quarters of them raised concerns about accounting-related guidance and reporting of TDRs.

Based on this information, regulatory officials from FDIC, the Federal Reserve, and OCC believe that the 2009 CRE loan workout guidance has been helpful.

Comments provided to regulatory officials during the examination process and through the formal appeals process provide information about banks' concerns on ratings and whether regulatory guidance has been applied consistently.

According to bank and regulatory officials with whom we spoke, when bank officials have raised concerns, they tend to first approach the examination team. Bank officials also can contact the ombudsman offices at the regulators to seek confidential assistance.[42]

In addition to these avenues, banks formally can appeal regulatory decisions. Although bankers have multiple options for raising concerns about regulatory actions, our interviews with bank officials found that some were cautious about raising issues because of potential repercussions from regulatory officials.[43]

In contrast, other bank officials stated that they do contact regulatory officials when warranted, although a few raised concerns about the time and expense of pursuing formal appeals.

Regulatory officials told us that many bank officials regularly reach out to them, and a few officials also noted that they provide information to bank officials about the ombudsman and the appeals process—should banks want to raise concerns.[44]

Banks' Concerns about Examiner Treatment of CRE Loans Highlight Challenges in Addressing CRE Downturn

Interviews with officials from 43 banks in different parts of the country identified multiple concerns with examiner treatment of CRE loans and related issues.[45] Many bank officials' overarching concern was that examiners have been applying guidance more stringently than before the financial crisis—a shift that a few bankers commented was a difficult adjustment.

Loan Classifications and Effect on Earnings

Some bank officials we interviewed expressed concerns with examiner-required loan classifications. From the perspective of a few bank officials we interviewed, a loan is performing when the borrower continues to pay and should not be classified. However, according to regulatory guidance and statements of regulatory officials, such a loan may be classified if identified weaknesses suggest a reduction in the borrower's capacity to repay that in turn could lead to future nonpayment. According to bankers and examiners with whom we spoke, "global cash flow" analysis always has been part of reviewing loans, but in the current economic downturn examiners have been focusing more closely on analysis and documentation of borrowers' and guarantors' global cash flows. The purpose of such analysis is to determine whether they have sufficient income and liquid assets to support loan payments. In some cases, such analysis shows that a borrower is unable to pay the loan, even if the borrower is currently paying. For example, the borrower's income and other debt obligations, when reviewed as a whole, could show that the borrower's debt obligations exceed income, which raises questions about whether the borrower will continue paying on the loan in the future.

The renewed focus on global cash flow analysis, in part, led many bank officials to conclude that examiners were classifying loans based either on collateral value or because the bank lacked updated financial statements. Regulatory field staff acknowledged that global cash flow analysis can be difficult to conduct because borrowers sometimes do not provide banks with updated financial statements. However, regulatory officials told us that examiners do not classify loans solely because of a lack of financial statements, but a lack of such statements combined with other weaknesses could provide sufficient support for classifying a loan. If the borrower lacks the ability to repay, the loan then could be considered "collateral dependent." Such loans are classified based on the value of the property, and tend to rely on values established in appraisals. According to some bank officials we interviewed, examiners have been more critical of recent appraisals. For example, these officials stated that examiners have been requiring appraisals on CRE collateral more often, criticizing the banks' appraisal review process, and criticizing the appraisals themselves.

Classifications are a major concern for banks primarily because they can result in reduced earnings. For example, an examiner may determine that a bank should place a classified loan on nonaccrual—which means the bank cannot accrue the interest income as earnings. While some bankers put loans on nonaccrual themselves, a few bank officials with whom we spoke stated that examiners have been asking bankers to place more loans on nonaccrual. Classifications also can reduce earnings because they factor into ALLL, which a bank estimates based on accounting guidance from the Financial Accounting Standards Board (FASB).[46] As more loans are classified, more is generally reserved in ALLL to anticipate future losses from nonperforming loans.[47] In our interviews with bank officials, some stated that examiners have been requiring additional ALLL and criticizing the ALLL methodology. In addition, a few bankers noted that some examiners want ALLL increased based on their peers' ALLL rather than the bank's individual situation.

Application of CRE-related Guidance

Many bank officials with whom we spoke were concerned that examiners have been misapplying the 2006 guidance. As we discuss above, the 2006 guidance states that the CRE and ADC concentration levels are not limits, but some bank officials told us that examiners have been interpreting them that way. A few bank officials also stated that examiners have not been calculating CRE concentrations according to the 2006 guidance: some examiners were including owner-occupied CRE and some were using the wrong type of capital for the calculation, which inflated the concentration levels (we also found this in our analysis, described in more detail below).[48] A few bankers stated that examiners told them they exceeded the 300 percent concentration threshold for CRE, based on these faulty calculations, but according to the calculations in the guidance they actually were under the threshold. Furthermore, a few bank officials also stated that it was unclear to them what examiners expect in complying with requirements related to CRE and risk management—for example, on what is considered to be satisfactory stress testing.

While more bank officials than not noted that examiners' actions have been consistent with the letter of the 2009 CRE loan workout guidance, a few stated that examiners were not always complying with its spirit: to allow the banks time to work with borrowers until the current CRE downturn passes.

Two bankers with whom we spoke stated that it was their experience that examiners were particularly stringent in 2008 when the financial crisis was escalating, but moderated their approach in late 2009, which is around the time that the 2009 CRE loan workout guidance was issued. An internal review by OCC's Midsize and Community Banks Division came to a similar conclusion and noted that examiners have become more consistent in their CRE loan treatment through internal discussions, training, and policy communication efforts.

A few bank officials with whom we spoke provided specific suggestions on how to improve policy guidance—such as clarifying what amount of debt service coverage is acceptable in a loan workout, how best to conduct global cash flow analysis, and when new appraisals are needed—but a few others felt that some form of general regulatory reprieve was needed for community banks to work through the downturn.

CAMELS and Capital Requirements

Bank officials we interviewed also stated that their experience with increased supervisory scrutiny was being reflected in CAMELS ratings and additional capital requirements. For example, many bank officials thought the management component rating was more critically assessed now, and heavily driven by asset quality and other component ratings.

A few bank officials added that they were being rated on deterioration in their portfolios that was due to the broader economic downturn and problems in their geographic market that were out of their control.

Some bank officials with whom we spoke stated that examiners have been more aggressive about requiring additional capital—and two bank officials in particular stated they thought this was especially the case for banks with high CRE concentrations.

However, a few bankers thought the additional scrutiny was appropriate, but should not necessarily be focused on all banks. For example, one banker stated that if examiners had been applying the guidance stringently before the crisis that perhaps the banks could have avoided some of the current problems.

A few others also noted that stricter scrutiny was appropriate given the current CRE market situation and the severity of the economic downturn. Additionally, a few bank officials stated that the regulators should focus on the community banks that caused the problems, rather than subjecting all community banks to such strict scrutiny.

Regulators Have Incorporated Lessons Learned from the Financial Crisis into Supervision, Which May Explain Some Bank Officials' Experiences of Increased Scrutiny

Regulators have been incorporating into their regulatory processes a number of lessons learned from the financial crisis, including findings from the agencies' IGs. Specifically, the IGs of the banking regulators completed 106 MLRs in 2009 and 2010 for banks that failed during the recent financial crisis.[49]

As noted in a December 2010 report by the FDIC IG that summarizes certain MLR findings, FDIC determined based on the MLRs that earlier supervisory action was needed to address banks with high risk profiles or weak risk-management practices. We also found in past work that regulators identified a number of weaknesses in institutions' risk-management systems before the financial crisis began but did not always take forceful actions to address them.[50]

In addition, the Financial Crisis Inquiry Commission report notes areas in which regulators could have been more proactive in using regulatory tools to address certain risks in the financial system.[51] A number of nonmanagement regulatory staff in the field offices we visited acknowledged they could have better followed up on outstanding issues.

In response to lessons learned, regulatory officials stated that they have been following up more often on matters requiring attention (MRA) and refocusing their supervisory efforts. For example, OCC's Midsize and Community Banks Division issued an MRA Reference Guide that provides examiners with OCC policy guidance on how to report, follow up on, and keep records related to MRAs.

FDIC in June 2009 also implemented its "Forward Looking Supervision" program that re-emphasizes reviewing all aspects of a bank's risks during the examination process.

The program focuses on helping ensure that (1) CAMELS ratings reflect consideration of bank management practices without relying solely on a bank's financial condition; (2) examiners review risks associated with concentrations and wholesale funding sources; (3) appropriate capital is maintained; and (4) examiners follow up on progress related to MRAs and enforcement actions.

Although Most Examinations We Reviewed Followed CRE Guidance, a Few Illustrated How Treatment of CRE Concentrations May Be Inconsistent

Based on our analysis of a nonprobability sample of 55 ROEs, examiners' findings were generally consistent with policy guidance, with some exceptions. Examiners made statements in ROEs related to the quality of banks' loan workouts that were consistent with the 2009 guidance on CRE loan workouts.[52] ROEs in our sample that comment broadly on banks' CRE loan workouts tend to cite areas for improvement (20 of 27). Examiner concerns include that the bank management or its board could have better identified, monitored, or tracked problem loan workouts, and therefore better identified loans that should have been reported as TDRs.

Improvements to managing loan workouts that examiners cited include (1) reporting on current loan status and related developments (such as periodic analysis of the borrower's financial situation); (2) creating and tracking benchmarks to measure workout progress; (3) providing the rationale for loan grades related to loan workouts; and (4) updating collateral values (as appropriate). Almost half of the ROEs in our sample that raise concerns related to CRE loan workouts (8 of 20) specifically note concerns about the nature of banks' loan workouts. For example, in these cases, examiners most often stated that loans were restructured and extended on unsustainable terms that either resulted in further asset quality deterioration, did not adequately assess the borrower's ability to repay, or did not follow the 2009 CRE loan workout guidance.

In our sample, most ROEs (44 of 55 sampled) raise concerns about CRE concentrations and how they are managed. In more than half of those (24 of 44), the concerns are supported by risk-management deficiencies and explicitly cite the 2006 CRE concentration guidance. Specifically, the findings include concerns on the bank's (1) need to update or enhance internal policies on CRE concentration limits and CRE underwriting acceptable to the bank; (2) monitoring of CRE concentrations; (3) management information systems used to track and report various types of CRE; (4) ability to inform the bank's board of directors about trends in CRE concentrations; and (5) the adequacy of stress testing of CRE loans.

However, in 7 instances (of 44), the ROE includes statements that the bank must reduce its CRE concentrations, but the basis for this requirement was unclear or appeared inconsistent with the 2006 CRE concentration guidance.[53]

For example:

- One ROE states that the bank needed to match its own internal policy on CRE concentrations to those in the 2006 guidance, and referred to the concentrations in the guidance as "limits." Referring to the thresholds in the 2006 guidance as limits is inconsistent with that guidance.
- In two other instances the ROEs state that the bank must reduce its CRE concentrations—citing them as "excessive" for example—but do not focus on the bank's risk-management systems. However, the enforcement actions for these banks did not require reduced CRE concentrations and emphasized improvements to risk management. One of these ROEs states repeatedly that the bank must reduce its CRE concentrations because the concentrations were too high "in the view of" the regulator. The related enforcement action did not require reduced CRE concentrations explicitly but required that the board "refine the concentration risk-management system" in part by establishing its own limits for certain CRE concentrations and adhering to them.[54] Differences in message between an ROE and an enforcement action could be confusing to bank boards and management as they seek to comply with regulatory requirements for risk management related to CRE concentrations. Moreover, such confusion could lead bank officials to misunderstand whether they should focus on improving their risk-management systems or just reduce their total CRE concentration numbers.
- Another ROE acknowledges that the bank was below the CRE threshold indicated in the 2006 guidance but states the bank nonetheless should follow the guidance and assesses in detail the bank's compliance with it. If banks are closely assessed on their compliance with the 2006 CRE guidance, although they have not reached the CRE and ADC thresholds, bank officials could be unclear on what the trigger is for compliance with CRE risk-management requirements.
- One case in particular provided ambiguous information to the bank about whether it had the appropriate risk-management systems in place to manage its CRE concentrations. The ROE requires a bank with a CRE concentration of about 600 percent of tier 1 capital to address a matter requiring immediate attention to improve stress testing for its CRE portfolio. The ROE also states that the bank

needed to reduce its CRE concentrations. However, the ROE states that the bank was in compliance with the 2006 CRE guidance—which requires robust stress testing for CRE portfolios when banks reach certain levels of CRE. Requiring a bank to address a matter requiring immediate attention related to CRE risk management and noting that the bank must reduce its CRE concentrations—while also stating that it is complying with the 2006 guidance—could send an unclear message to bank officials about why they need to reduce CRE concentrations if overall they are complying with the guidance.

Additionally, we found that out of 47 ROEs that include CRE concentration information, a number of them did not include CRE concentration numbers that were calculated according to the 2006 CRE guidance.

For example, some ROEs appear to include owner-occupied CRE as part of the CRE concentration calculation (14 of 47), although the 2006 CRE guidance specifically excludes this type of CRE. We also found that 23 of these 47 ROEs include CRE concentrations calculated by using some combination of tier 1 capital (and sometimes also include a number simply referred to as a "concentration," although how it was calculated was unclear). However, another 24 ROEs specify using either total risk- based capital or equity capital (or also include tier 1 capital), which is consistent with the 2006 guidance.[55]

The effect of calculating these concentrations differently can be to increase the total CRE concentration number, which increases the scrutiny placed on the banks' risk- management systems.

Sometimes the difference can be large: one ROE in our sample that includes both calculations shows a total CRE concentration of 432 percent when using tier 1 capital and 341 percent when using total risk-based capital. However, the difference also can be smaller: one ROE in our sample has a concentration calculated with tier 1 capital at 141 percent; with total risk-based capital it was 133 percent.

While FDIC clarified to its examiners in April 2010 how to calculate CRE concentrations, other regulators have not done so. Moreover, two of the FDIC ROEs in our sample that use only tier 1 capital in the calculation were issued after the April 2010 clarification.

Regulatory Officials' Differing Views on the Adequacy of the 2006 CRE Concentration Guidance Could Lead to Inconsistent Treatment of CRE Loans

Senior officials and field examiners have differing views on whether the 2006 CRE guidance is sufficient in addressing CRE concentration risks. We interviewed about 200 field staff associated with the bank examination review process at FDIC, the Federal Reserve, and OCC in Atlanta, Boston, Dallas, and San Francisco.[56] A number of field examiners from all the agencies stated they did not have the tools to proactively address growing CRE concentrations when the economy was strong or that some banks ignored examiners' concerns on CRE risk management. A number of examiners also admitted that during strong economic times they could have been more assertive in asking banks to implement risk-management changes related to CRE concentrations. When asked whether limits on CRE concentrations should be considered or whether specific amounts of capital should be required at certain concentration levels, some examiners did not think that limits were the answer, but others thought that there might be some level of concentration that was too high even when managed well, because a market downturn would expose banks to significant losses. In addition, some thought that a focus on additional capital would be sensible given the severe capital shortfalls some banks with CRE concentrations faced during the financial crisis.

Senior regulatory officials with whom we spoke had differing views on whether the 2006 guidance was sufficient for examiners to address the buildup in CRE concentration risks. FDIC senior officials stated that the current guidance was sufficient for examiners to address risks related to CRE concentrations and did not think changes were needed. In contrast, OCC has been reviewing whether particular capital requirements should be set for banks that have higher CRE concentrations and stated that this could lead to changes in OCC or interagency guidance. At the Federal Reserve, senior officials believed that the existing 2006 guidance was largely sufficient, but noted that efforts to clarify expectations for stress testing and capital planning were ongoing. The examiners and senior officials with whom we spoke agreed that determining certain limits on CRE concentrations, or requiring specific amounts of additional capital for certain levels of CRE concentrations, would be difficult and require significant study. Federal Reserve officials also noted that limits or specific capital requirements would require studies on the potential effect on credit availability. Examiners exercise significant judgment during examinations, and different perceptions about the 2006 guidance among regulators could send mixed signals to examiners—which could affect how they apply the guidance.

In addition, as noted earlier, the regulators' processes to review and monitor application of examiner guidance and our review of ROEs identified some inconsistencies.

Monitoring and revising existing controls, such as guidance, is a key component of a strong internal control system and reflects management's efforts to implement findings from quality control processes.

MULTIPLE FACTORS CAN AFFECT BANKS' LENDING DECISIONS, INCLUDING REGULATORS' ACTIONS

Capital Requirements Can Affect Lending

Regulators require banks to maintain certain minimum capital requirements to help ensure the safety and soundness of the banking system. However, increases in capital requirements can raise the cost of providing loans, which would lead to higher interest rates for borrowers, tighter credit terms, or reduced lending. While capital provides an important cushion against losses for banks, there is a trade-off between building up this cushion to provide greater protection against unexpected losses and increasing lending and returns to shareholders. Holding more capital against each loan means less equity is available to return to shareholders or back new loans.[57]

Empirical literature generally supports this basic understanding of the impact of bank capital requirements on lending. For example, researchers found in one study that bank capital requirements substantially affected bank loan growth during the last economic downturn.

Specifically, in evaluating bank regulatory agreements in New England, researchers found that capital requirements significantly affected the lending behavior of banks. They noted that those banks with "low or no profits and an inability to obtain new capital at reasonable rates" decreased their assets and liabilities to meet the higher capital-to-asset ratios required by regulatory enforcement actions.[58]

Using the "capital crunch hypothesis," the researchers found that institutions with lower capital ratios had slower loan growth (or loans shrank more rapidly) to try to satisfy capital requirements.[59]

High Concentrations in CRE Can Inhibit Banks' Ability to Lend, Especially during a Credit Downturn

Banks with capital bases that have been negatively affected by losses in their CRE portfolios—or those trying to improve their capital ratios or ALLL to guard against potential losses—may need to reduce lending to maintain an adequate capital-to-assets ratio on their balance sheets. Although limited research exists on the impact of CRE loan concentrations on a bank's ability to lend, an existing study shows that high CRE concentrations can limit loan growth during economic downturns. For example, this study found that banks with high CRE concentrations before the recent financial crisis made loans to other sectors of the economy during this crisis at a "significantly slower rate" than banks that did not have high CRE exposure.[60] In addition, the researchers found that the higher the bank's CRE concentration prior to the crisis, the more its non-CRE lending slowed during the crisis.

The reasons for the contraction of non-CRE lending during the crisis are being examined. The authors hypothesize that the rise in CRE lending and the substantially increased delinquencies on these loans "could have inhibited banks' willingness or ability to lend to other segments of the economy—particularly when banks' demand for liquidity and capital was high." The authors also cite the possibility that high-CRE banks may have failed at a greater rate than banks without that level of CRE exposure.

Limited Research from Past Downturns on the Effect of Examiner Actions on Lending Suggests It Is Minimal

Our assessment of existing studies and interviews with bank officials found that market factors tend to drive CRE downturns and suggests that the regulatory effect of examiner actions on such downturns—as evidenced in studies of the downturn of the 1990s—was minimal. Bankers we interviewed attributed the CRE downturn to market factors such as problems in residential real estate that affected the CRE market and the severity of the broader financial and economic crisis. Although bankers did not state that regulatory policies were the cause of the CRE downturn, many noted that examiner actions were exacerbating it and a few stated banks needed to be given time to work through their troubled assets so they could continue to lend and support the economy. Other bankers stated that examiners have been impeding banks' ability to make new loans—especially if the bank already had high CRE concentrations. That said, a few bankers noted that CRE loan demand from creditworthy borrowers was down significantly, and this was inhibiting loan growth.

There is limited research on the effect of examiner actions on credit cycles; however, the studies that exist suggest the effects are minimal. Specifically:

- In an analysis of the credit crunch from 1989 to 1992, researchers found modest support for the hypothesis that increased regulatory "toughness" occurred and that this affected bank lending. In a comprehensive study spanning the last financial crisis, three hypotheses were tested regarding changes in regulatory toughness and its impact on bank lending.[61] The data provided what the authors call modest support for all three hypotheses that: (1) toughness increased during the credit crunch from 1989 through 1992, (2) it declined during the boom from 1993 through 1998, and (3) differences in toughness affected bank lending. During the credit crunch they studied, the data show no more than 1 percent additional loans receiving classification or worsening of classification status. During the boom, the data show a similar change for a decrease in loan classifications. The authors also reviewed the economic significance of changes in regulatory "toughness" and found that growth in the number of classified assets by 1 percent would be predicted to decrease the ratio of real estate loans to gross total assets by less than 1 percentage point over the long term, and frequently this impact was projected to be significantly less than 1 percentage point. Changes in CAMEL ratings were not found to have a "consistent" impact on future lending behavior, and when there was an impact, the data show that it was minimal.[62]
- Another article specifically focuses on how changes in CAMEL ratings affected loan growth from the period that spanned 1985–2004.[63] During the 1985–1993 credit crunch, the authors found some evidence that changes in CAMEL ratings, both the composite and the components, had a significant impact on loan growth for commercial and industrial loans but a smaller effect on consumer loans and real estate loans.[64] However, the authors found minimal evidence that adjustments in CAMEL ratings, including both composite and component ratings, had any systematic effect on loan growth during what they define as an economic recovery period (1994–2004). The

researchers also noted that, based on their research, banks may respond "asymmetrically" to changes in CAMEL ratings. Specifically, banks may decrease loan growth when their CAMEL ratings are downgraded, but they do not necessarily increase it when their CAMEL ratings are upgraded.

These studies suggest examiners' actions can affect lending, albeit minimally. However, the research suggests that regulators were more stringent during the past credit crunch, even holding financial conditions constant. Therefore, regulators should be aware of how their actions can affect broader credit markets, and help ensure that their actions do not contribute to unnecessary procyclical effects: that is, magnification of economic or financial fluctuations.

Regulators Are Aware of the Need to Moderate the Potential Procyclical Effects of Regulation

In the aftermath of the recent financial crisis, regulators in the United States and abroad have been attempting to address the procyclical effects of their actions. The procyclical effects of regulation may not adequately discourage overly risky behavior during economic upswings or may inhibit bank lending during downturns, as banks may need to meet more stringent requirements during times when it is more difficult to do so. For instance, if regulators increase capital requirements at the same time that losses from an economic downturn decrease banks' capital, banks may be less able to lend while they seek to rapidly raise additional capital. This can exacerbate downswings in credit cycles.

Consistent and balanced application of policy guidance in strong and weak economic times is important to avoiding unnecessary procyclical effects. Regulatory efforts to better ensure that guidance is applied consistently during strong and weak economic periods helps to ensure that regulatory policies do not exacerbate economic upturns or downturns.[65] While bankers with whom we spoke understood why examiners were looking more closely at CRE loans given the market's downturn, a few said the shift to closer review and attention was a difficult adjustment. Bank examiners with whom we spoke in the field offices also noted that problems can be difficult to identify during strong economic times.

Discussions about the procyclicality of regulation have been a central feature of recent deliberations on revised capital requirements among U.S.

banking regulators and the Basel Committee for Banking Supervision. The discussions have been seeking to address the procyclical effects of capital requirements by having banks raise additional capital, commensurate with risks, during times of economic growth.

In December 2010, the Basel Committee released the framework for Basel III, which includes increased and higher-quality capital requirements, enhanced risk coverage, the establishment of a leverage ratio as a "backstop" to the risk-based requirement, steps to encourage the "build up" of capital that can be used to absorb losses during "periods of stress," and the introduction of two global liquidity standards.

As part of the establishment of procedures to help ensure the consistent global application of this framework, the Basel Committee has developed standards that will be implemented gradually so that banks make the shift to higher capital and liquidity standards while "supporting lending to the economy."[66]

Federal bank regulators also have acknowledged the importance of addressing procyclicality in regulatory requirements and have made efforts in this regard. For example, the Chairman of the Federal Reserve has stated the importance of regulators acknowledging the significance of procyclicality and he has noted that both the Basel Committee and the Financial Stability Forum have worked to address this as it relates to capital requirements. In addition, FASB has issued accounting guidance aimed at changes to mark-to-market accounting for assessing asset values in inactive markets. More recently, in May 2010, FASB released a proposed Accounting Standards Update, which encompassed proposals on the impairment of financial assets and suggested implementing a more forward-looking impairment model.[67]

Based on exposure draft comments, in January 2011 FASB proposed with the International Accounting Standards Board a common solution on how to account for the impairment of financial assets and presented the document for public comment. Efforts such as these seek to address procyclicality concerns related to capital and accounting requirements, while the potential procyclical effects of examiners' application of policy guidance is something regulators consider in their supervision of banks, according to regulatory officials with whom we spoke.

The recent financial crisis underscored how important it is for regulators to evenly apply guidance during strong economic periods, although this was not always the case, as previously noted. Consistent application of guidance is important to avoid unduly hampering credit provision throughout the economy.

Conclusion

CRE still is working through a downturn sparked by the broader financial crisis, presenting an ongoing challenge to community banks and regulators. While community banks have been working through the challenges associated with many years of past growth in CRE concentrations, CRE portfolios continue to have a significant effect on community bank balance sheets as loan delinquencies and charge-offs remain historically high. Community banks continue to seek ways to work with their borrowers and shore up capital to remain solvent, but the current economic environment and the expectation that refinancing of CRE loans will bring a new round of market stress suggest many community banks may face these challenges for some time. And, because community banks tend to provide a greater proportion of their loans to small businesses, the availability of credit to small businesses could be constrained while community banks work through these difficulties.

Prior to the financial crisis, regulators' efforts included guidance on CRE concentrations and risk management, but these efforts were not as robust as they could have been in addressing CRE risks. Since the financial crisis, the shift in examination focus and differences in the application of the CRE concentration guidance has contributed to concerns among community banks about regulatory stringency. That is, a number of bankers remain concerned that regulators have become more stringent in reviewing CRE loans since the crisis, which could be explained partly by regulators re-emphasizing fundamentals and addressing lessons learned from the crisis. While we and the regulators have reviewed examiner application of the CRE guidance and generally found examiners' actions were accurate or well-supported, some inaccuracies and inconsistencies were evident—particularly relating to the 2006 guidance. Regulators have mixed views about the adequacy of the 2006 guidance. Our findings from an analysis of ROEs were similar to those of the regulators' internal reviews and assessments, which raised questions about the consistency of policy guidance application. Given these findings, and in light of lessons learned from the recent financial crisis and CRE market downturn, the regulators could reassess the adequacy of the guidance. Revising or supplementing the guidance to provide more details about risk- management practices and examples of when to reduce CRE concentrations would help both examiners and bankers better understand how to assess and manage such concentrations. Furthermore, incorporating CRE-specific analyses into the scope of internal and quality assurance reviews—at least while CRE issues remain a concern—will help ensure consistent application of the guidance and produce clearly articulated support in examination reports for requiring reduced concentrations. In this way, regulatory management can better ensure that examination practices related to CRE concentrations and risks will be carried out consistently from examiner to examiner and across regulators. Consistent treatment also will make clear to banks what regulatory expectations are for managing CRE concentration risks.

Given the key role community banks play in business lending, bank regulators are aware of the potential effects of their actions in exacerbating the credit cycle. Many factors can affect a bank's decision to lend, including regulatory requirements. But if such requirements are too stringent, they can unduly limit lending. Such limits on lending can have widespread effects on the economy, as acknowledged in Basel Committee for Banking Supervision discussions on capital requirements. Although isolating the impact of bank supervision is difficult, the recent severe cycle of credit upswings followed by the downturn serves as a useful reminder of the supervisory balance needed to help ensure the safety and soundness of the banking system and support economic recovery.

RECOMMENDATIONS FOR EXECUTIVE ACTION

To improve supervision of CRE-related risks, we recommend that the Chairman of the Federal Deposit Insurance Corporation, the Chairman of the Board of Governors of the Federal Reserve System, and the Comptroller of the Currency:

- Enhance and either re-issue or supplement interagency CRE concentration guidance—based on agreed-upon standards by FDIC, the Federal Reserve, and OCC—to provide greater clarity and more examples to help banks comply with CRE concentration and risk-management requirements and help examiners ensure consistency in their application of the guidance, especially related to reductions in CRE concentrations and calculation of CRE concentrations.
- After issuing revised or supplemental CRE concentration guidance, incorporate steps in existing review and quality assurance processes, as appropriate, to better ensure that the revised guidance is implemented consistently and that examiners clearly indicate within bank examination reports the basis for requiring a bank to reduce CRE loan concentrations.

Agency Comments and Our Evaluation

We provided a draft of this report to FDIC, the Federal Reserve, and OCC for review and comment. All of the agencies provided written comments. The agencies also provided technical comments, which we considered and have incorporated as appropriate.

In written comments, the Federal Reserve welcomed our recommendations to improve CRE concentrations guidance to help banks and examiners comply with it, and to ensure consistent implementation of such guidance. The Federal Reserve stated that it intends to work with its counterparts at the OCC and FDIC to develop and implement enhancements to CRE concentrations guidance.

In its written comments, the OCC agreed with our conclusions and recommendations. OCC noted that community banks' increased CRE concentrations exposes them to CRE market declines, which may require more explicit regulatory expectations for the robustness of risk- management systems, stress testing, capital planning, and capital levels when CRE concentrations increase. OCC also stated that it would discuss with the other federal banking regulators how to enhance the 2006 CRE concentrations guidance and would ensure the consistent implementation of any revised or supplemented guidance.

In written comments, FDIC stated that it has already supplemented the 2006 CRE concentrations and risk-management guidance—citing a 2008 Financial Institution Letter, divisionwide training, and internal reviews. As noted in our report, the federal banking regulators all have numerous controls to help ensure examination consistency, such as training and internal reviews that FDIC highlights in its letter. Nonetheless, our review of ROEs from all three regulators, and their own internal reviews, uncovered instances of inconsistency in the treatment of CRE loans and application of the 2006 CRE guidance—demonstrating that no regulator was immune from consistency issues. We also noted in our report some concerns raised by bank examiners and bankers about applying the 2006 guidance, such as whether the current CRE concentration thresholds are hard limits, how the CRE concentrations should be calculated, and whether specific amounts of additional capital should be required for banks with elevated CRE concentrations. Though FDIC provided clarification on CRE risk management in March 2008 that could contribute to interagency action on CRE guidance, this guidance does not address all of the concerns raised more recently by examiners and bankers that we describe in the report, nor was it developed in conjunction with the other regulators. Therefore, we continue to believe that our recommendations on enhanced or clarified CRE concentration guidance—on an interagency basis that involves the FDIC—would help bankers and examiners better understand how to comply with CRE risk management requirements and help ensure the consistent application of such requirements.

FDIC also cited a study by the Bank for International Settlements that concluded the social benefits of higher bank capital requirements outweigh the large reductions in economic activity from a banking collapse. As our report notes, additional capital provides an important cushion against losses, though this comes at a cost. From our review of the literature, there is disagreement on the magnitude of such costs on lending. We added information to the report to clarify this issue, which includes information on the study cited by FDIC.

Sincerely yours,

A. Nicole Clowers
Acting Director
Financial Markets and Community Investment

Appendix I. Scope and Methodology

To assess the condition of the commercial real estate (CRE) market and the implications for community banks, we collected and analyzed the following data to provide information on overall trends in CRE:

- To determine trends in CRE prices, we analyzed monthly data from Moody's/REAL Commercial Property Price Index from January 2002 through December 2010. We assessed their reliability for the purposes of providing a picture of the trends in CRE prices by reviewing documentation on how the data were collected and reviewed for accuracy. We determined that the data were sufficiently reliable for the purpose of determining price trends.
- To determine when CRE loans would be up for refinancing and what percentage of CRE loans were "underwater," we analyzed data on CRE loan volume by maturity schedule and underlying collateral value provided by Trepp, a commercial mortgage analysis firm. To determine the accuracy of these data, we discussed the data with officials and reviewed documentation on their data quality processes. We determined that the data was sufficiently reliable for purposes of

determining when CRE loans were maturing and how many were underwater.

To understand how the condition of the CRE market has affected community banks, we analyzed call report data from the Federal Deposit Insurance Corporation (FDIC) for banks with assets of less than $1 billion to assess (1) CRE loan concentrations as a percent of total loans and leases, (2) trends in CRE loan concentrations as a percent of total risk- based capital, (3) trends in CRE loans that were noncurrent, and (4) trends in CRE loans charged off. We assessed changes in the rate of noncurrent CRE loans and CRE loan charge-offs over time. We also calculated average CRE concentration rates at community banks from 1996 through 2010 by taking the aggregate reported total of loans secured by CRE (the sum of construction and development, nonfarm nonresidential, and multifamily residential real estate) divided by the reported amount of total risk-based capital. We conducted similar analyses for commercial banks with assets more than $1 billion. We assessed the reliability of the call report data by reviewing the controls in place to help ensure its accuracy and by relying on past GAO reviews of these data. We determined that they were sufficiently reliable for the purpose of determining trends in CRE loan concentrations and performance at community banks.

Reports by the inspectors general of the federal banking regulators provided additional information on the effect of the CRE market downturn on community banks. We reviewed all 106 of the material loss reviews (MLR) issued by the offices of the inspectors general of the Board of Governors of the Federal Reserve System (Federal Reserve), FDIC, and U.S. Department of the Treasury (for the Office of the Comptroller of the Currency, or OCC) from 2009 and 2010. In reviewing the MLRs, we noted which ones cited concentrations in either overall CRE or acquisition, development, and construction loans (ADC) as a factor in the bank's failure. We also interviewed officials at the Conference of State Bank Regulators on the findings of their independent review of the MLRs.

Additional reports provided background and information on the overall condition of CRE markets and their impact on community banks. The reports we reviewed were culled from research and literature reviews from academic journals, the Congressional Research Service, the Congressional Oversight Panel, FDIC, the Federal Reserve, and previous GAO reports. We also spoke with and reviewed speeches and public comments from officials at FDIC, the Federal Reserve, and OCC; bank officials; and academics and a think tank official with expertise on bank examinations or CRE.

To determine how the banking regulators responded to trends in the CRE market, we interviewed regulatory and bank officials and reviewed reports of examination (ROE) from a sample of banks.[68] Our sample selection for bank interviews and reviews of ROEs started with a data request to FDIC, the Federal Reserve, and OCC on bank examinations for banks with assets of less than $1 billion with data elements that included the value of their CRE loans, recent CAMELS ratings, total risk-based capital, recent enforcement actions, and other information.[69] We determined that the data were sufficiently reliable for the purposes of selecting a sample, based on prior use of these data and interviews with agency officials. We further refined the sample so that we would have a breadth of banks for interviews and ROE reviews, based on the state in which they were located, their CAMELS composite rating, and their regulator. We also wanted to increase the likelihood that banks we sampled were relevant to our study; therefore, we selected banks with elevated CRE and ADC concentrations and those that had a recent bank examination. To achieve these goals, we selected the sample as follows.

- From the bank examination information we received from the regulators, we selected banks from California, Georgia, Massachusetts, and Texas. We selected these states because the banks in the first two states have had a relatively greater share of CRE-related nonperforming loans, and the latter two states a relatively smaller share of such loans (as measured by the percentage of CRE loans past due or in nonaccrual).[70] We also wanted to include states from different regions of the country. To inform the selection, we conducted an analysis of call report data downloaded from SNL Financial and held discussions with the federal banking regulators. We analyzed the following data points for commercial banks with assets of less than or equal to $1 billion: (1) loans and leases for construction and land development, multifamily, owner-occupied real estate, other property, and nonfarm nonresidential; (2) loans 90 days past due for each of these categories; and (3) loans in nonaccrual status for each of these categories. We reviewed these commercial banks in each of the 50 states in relation to these measures and total assets in CRE loan categories, and arrived at our four states. We reviewed SNL data reliability and determined that it was sufficient for the purposes of selecting states for our sample.
- We further refined the sample to include only banks that had an examination conducted after October 2009, to capture those

examinations for which the 2009 CRE loan workout guidance would have applied.[71]

- From that subset, we placed banks into four "pools," with the goal of speaking with officials from, and reviewing ROEs for, a breadth of community banks from a range of states in our sample, from all three of the banking regulators, and with a range of CAMELS ratings.
  - **Pool 1** consisted of banks with good CAMELS composite ratings and high CRE concentrations. In this group, we included banks with a CAMELS composite rating of 1 or 2 and a CRE concentration above 300 percent of CRE loans (including owner-occupied) to total capital. By including owner-occupied loans, we would ensure the largest possible pool of banks and also identify concerns that such banks might have about regulatory treatment of their CRE loans.
  - **Pool 2** consisted of banks that generally were in good condition but also had ADC concentrations. Pool 2 criteria were a CAMELS composite rating of 2 and both a 300 percent or greater concentration in overall CRE and a 100 percent or greater concentration in ADC loans to total capital.
  - **Pool 3** banks were intended to represent banks that were struggling and that had a higher number of loans classified as loss at the most recent examination. These had a CAMELS composite rating of 3, an overall CRE concentration of 300 percent or greater, and a proportion of loans classified loss to total assets in the 75th percentile and above, for banks within our sample. This "loss ratio" was calculated by taking the total assets classified loss for the most recent examination and dividing them by total assets.
  - **Pool 4** was the most distressed pool of banks and consisted of banks with CAMELS composite ratings of 4 or 5, a 300 percent or greater concentration in overall CRE in the 75th percentile or greater for the banks in our sample, and a loss ratio in the 75th percentile of our sample, calculated as described above.
- Once we selected these pools, we began contacting banks to interview. We simultaneously began requesting ROEs and some related workpapers from the federal banking regulators. In that process, we learned that FDIC and Federal Reserve data included ROEs led by the state banking regulator (because they share

examination responsibilities with state examiners), and we excluded these from our sample.

The resulting sample from this process is outlined below, broken down by regulator (table 5), state (table 6), and CAMELS ratings (table 7). OCC-supervised banks represent the greatest number of banks in our sample, in part because a number of the examinations in our sample for the Federal Reserve and FDIC were led by the state regulator and were out of the scope of our review. To avoid overweighting the sample with OCC- supervised banks, we randomly removed some OCC-led bank examinations for which we had a sufficient number of cases: banks rated 2 in Texas.

Table 5. Sample Selection by Regulator for ROE Analysis

Agency	**Number**	**Percent of total**
FDIC	21	38
Federal Reserve	12	22
OCC	22	40
Total	**55**	**100**

Source: GAO.

Table 6. Sample Selection by State for ROE Analysis

State	**Number**	**Percent of total**
California	16	29
Massachusetts	5	9
Georgia	12	22
Texas	22	40
Total	**55**	**100**
Total for Massachusetts plus Texas (fewer CRE problems)	**27**	**49**
Total for California plus Georgia (more CRE problems)	**28**	**51**

Source: GAO.

To further understand how FDIC, the Federal Reserve, and OCC have responded to the CRE downturn and its effect on community banks, we collected and analyzed interagency policy guidance to examiners related to

CRE loan treatment and interagency statements on lending, and also assessed regulatory efforts to address CRE-related concerns.

Table 7. Sample Selection by CAMELS Composite Rating for ROE Analysis

CAMELS composite rating	Number	Percent of total
CAMELS 1	4	7
CAMELS 2	24	44
CAMELS 3	14	25
CAMELS 4	3	5
CAMELS 5	10	18
Total	**55**	**100**
Total 1 and 2 rated	**28**	**51**
Total 3 rated	**14**	**26**
Total 4 and 5 rated	**13**	**24**

Source: GAO.

As part of this work, we observed examiner training at FFIEC provided to commissioned examiners, to include a week-long training on CRE and a day-long training on regulatory updates related to policy guidance on CRE loans.

To understand banks' concerns about examiners' treatment of their CRE loans and how examiners supported findings related to CRE loans, we interviewed bank and regulatory officials and analyzed ROEs.

- We spoke with community bank officials affiliated with 43 community banks in a number of states (see table 8). Most of the bank officials with whom we spoke were located in California, Georgia, and Texas based on our nonprobability sample. We initiated contact with 62 banks drawn from this sample and interviewed all of the 21 bank officials who responded to us. We gained additional bank views by supplementing this sample. Specifically, we interviewed officials from 22 additional banks that either testified before Congress on the issue of CRE, were identified to us through bank associations, or had learned of our work and wanted to talk to us. When we summarize statements from our interviews with bank officials throughout this report, we use the term "a few" to refer to 3–10 of 43 banks making the statement; "some" to refer to 11–25 of 43 banks making the statement; and "many" to refer to 26–43 banks making a statement.

We do not provide specific numbers in the body of the report to avoid overstating the precision of the results from the nonprobability sample we used to select bank interviewees.

- We interviewed more than 230 regulatory field staff at FDIC, throughout the Federal Reserve System, and at OCC—along with additional staff at these regulators' headquarters—to seek views and information about recent practices on CRE-specific guidance related to loan workouts and concentrations, training provided on the guidance, CAMELS ratings, capital requirements, and liquidity issues. The interviews were conducted at headquarters offices in Washington, D.C., and by telephone, video teleconference, and in person at district, regional, and field offices in California, Colorado, Georgia, Massachusetts, and Texas. We sought to determine if there were different views or practices related to CRE loan treatment among regulatory roles or between those in headquarters and the field offices, and therefore we interviewed staff in a range of roles and locations. The staff with whom we spoke in field locations included field examiners, their supervisors, case managers, analysts (at OCC), and senior management. Examiners were interviewed both in group settings and individually, and included those who served as examiners-in-charge (EIC) for ROEs in our sample. Examiners interviewed in group settings were gathered by the field offices, and based on our request, had a range of experience (either less than 5 years or more than 5 years, because examiners are usually commissioned within 5 years). Individual meetings with EICs were held based on our nonprobability sample. Of the field staff we interviewed, about 200 were directly involved in drafting or reviewing ROEs, and about 50 of the 200 were in senior management positions.
- We analyzed 55 ROEs based on our nonprobability sample, as described above, of banks in California, Georgia, Massachusetts, and Texas. We reviewed how examiners supported statements related to banks' CRE loan workouts, concerns about CRE concentrations, and how examiners calculated CRE concentrations.

To understand the controls the regulators have in place to help ensure consistent application of policy guidance, we reviewed the examination report review process at all of the regulators based on regulatory guidance and interviews with regulatory officials.

Table 8. Locations of Banks Whose Officials We Interviewed

	State															
	Calif.	**Fla.**	**Ga.**	**Ill.**	**Kan.**	**Mass.**	**Md.**	**Mich.**	**N.C.**	**N.J.**	**N.M.**	**Ohio**	**Ok.**	**S.C.**	**Tex**	**Wis.**
Banks	12	4	5	2	1	1	2	1	1	1	1	1	1	1	8	1

Source: GAO.

We also collected, compared, and analyzed examination review reports and quality assurance processes for the three regulators to determine what processes were in place to identify and address inconsistencies among examiners, and what findings had resulted from these reviews.

For FDIC, we reviewed reports conducted by FDIC's Internal Control and Review Section for the Atlanta, Dallas, New York, and San Francisco regions, because these regions covered the states in our nonprobability sample. For OCC, we reviewed reports from all four of its districts related to the agency's quality assurance process that focused on reviewing the classifications of CRE loans. For the Federal Reserve, we reviewed a special engagement report from the General Auditor at the Federal Reserve Bank of Atlanta and a Quality Assurance memorandum for the Atlanta, Kansas City, Philadelphia, and Richmond districts. We also discussed with Federal Reserve staff whether other similar studies existed.

To determine and assess the factors that can affect banks' lending decisions and their impact, we reviewed and summarized academic studies that included analysis of various factors on bank lending. With assistance from a research librarian, we conducted searches of research databases and report sources (Congressional Research Service, Congressional Budget Office, JSTOR, ProQuest, EconLit, Accounting and Tax Database, and Social Science Search). We also sought and reviewed studies cited by the American Bankers Association (ABA) and the Independent Community Bankers of America (ICBA).

All studies included published papers released between 1991 and 2010. Based on our selection criteria, we determined that six studies were sufficient for our purposes.

Specifically, with the assistance of a senior economist, we analyzed the methodologies underlying these studies and determined that they were the most relevant to our study and also had robust controls. Nonetheless, the research conducted in this area is not exhaustive and focuses primarily on what occurred during the previous economic downturn of the late 1980s and early 1990s. However, we did identify one study that examines the role of CRE and its effect on bank lending in the current financial crisis. To further demonstrate how loan losses, allowance for loan and lease losses, and capital requirements can affect lending, we developed an illustrative example of how loan losses affect capital ratios on a bank's balance sheet, with assistance from certified public accountants.

To obtain information on how examiner practices may affect lending, we interviewed bankers, examiners, and regulatory officials. We also interviewed officials from ABA, the Conference of State Bank Supervisors, and ICBA.

APPENDIX II. ALLL AND LOAN LOSS IMPACT ON CAPITAL

Increases in capital requirements or the allowance for loan and lease loss (ALLL) can affect a bank's ability to lend. Figure 6 illustrates relationships between loan losses, bank balance sheets, and capital requirements under certain assumptions.

In this simplified example, the bank begins with $1,000 in assets ($1,010 in loans and $10 in ALLL), $900 in liabilities, and $100 in capital, which equates to a total capital ratio of 10 percent (calculated by dividing total capital by total assets).[72] In this example the bank has analyzed the collectibility of its loans and decided to add $20 to its ALLL in anticipation of loan losses. Provisions for these losses increase the ALLL, which in turn are charged to the bank's expenses, reduce income, and therefore reduce retained earnings that are included as part of total capital. As a result, the capital ratio falls to 8.2 percent.

If the bank identifies as uncollectible and charges off a $20 loan that it holds as an asset, given the assumptions in the example, the bank's total loans and ALLL would each decline by $20 with no change in capital. If the bank conducts another analysis of its loan collectibility and decides to add to its ALLL, then its capital would be further reduced.

For this example, if the bank decides to—or is required to—meet a 10 percent capital ratio after adding to its ALLL to cover estimated future losses, it would need to raise capital by seeking it from the bank's owners or from investors.

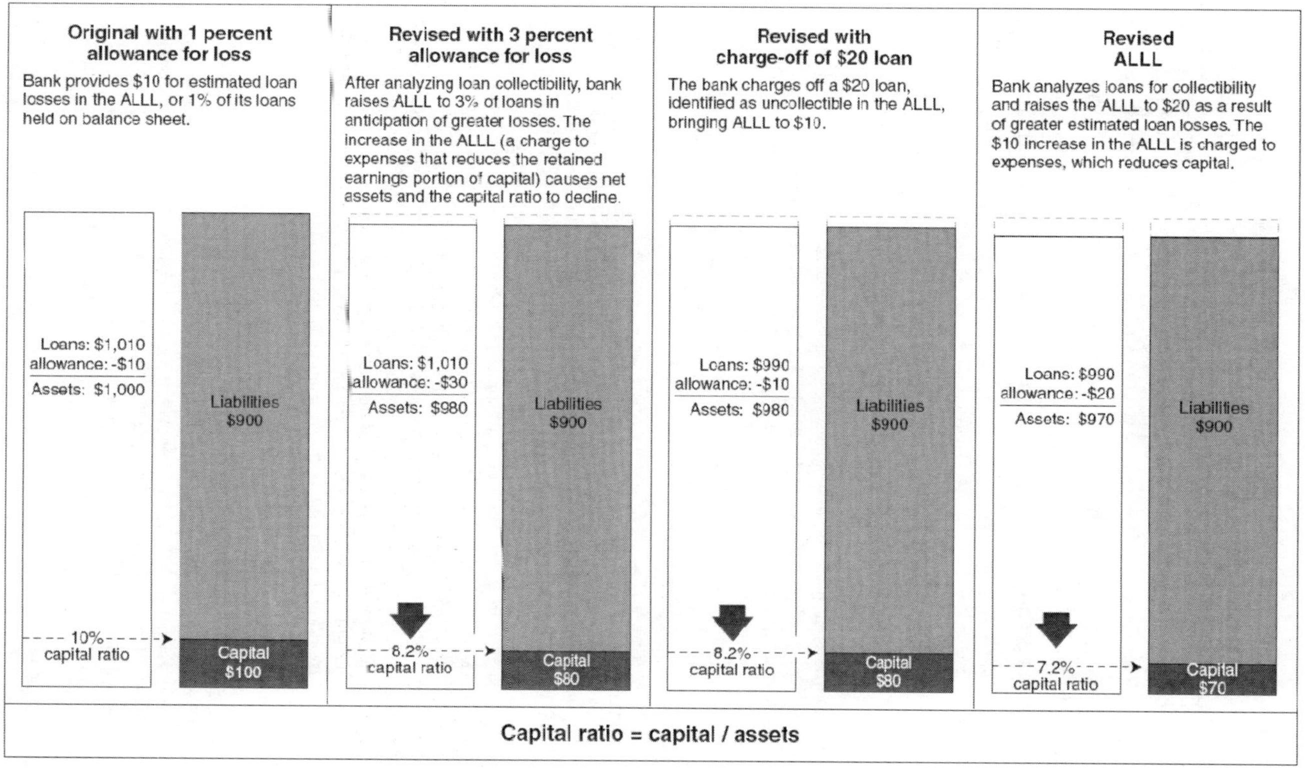

Source: GAO.

Figure 6. Illustration of How ALLL and Loan Losses Can Affect Capital Ratios on a Bank's Balance Sheet.

If the bank cannot raise additional capital because it is in poor financial condition, or chooses not to because the cost of capital is prohibitive, then it could, among other options, reduce its assets (perhaps by selling assets such as other real estate owned) to decrease liabilities or by paying off borrowings to increase the capital ratio. Reducing assets is often referred to as "shrinking the balance sheet." However, banks in better financial condition may be able to respond differently in the face of loan losses—they may be able to continue lending without raising additional capital or can rely on their stronger financial position to secure new capital.

End Notes

[1] Throughout this report we define community banks as banks regulated by a federal banking regulator that have $1 billion or less in total assets. Commercial real estate includes rental apartment buildings, industrial properties, office buildings, hotels, healthcare-related properties, and retail properties such as shopping malls, strip malls, and freestanding outlets.

[2] Capital generally is defined as a **firm's** long-term source of funding, contributed largely by a firm's equity stockholders and its own returns in the form of retained earnings. One important function of capital is to absorb losses.

[3] The interagency statements and guidance they issued from 2006 through 2010 are: OCC, Federal Reserve, and FDIC, *Concentrations in Commercial Real Estate Lending, Sound Risk Management Practices,* 71 Fed. Reg. 74580 (Dec. 12, 2006); FDIC, Federal Reserve, OCC, and the Office of Thrift Supervision (OTS), *Interagency Statement on Meeting the Needs of Creditworthy Borrowers* (Nov. 12, 2008); FDIC, Federal Reserve, OCC, OTS, the National Credit Union Administration (NCUA), and the Federal Financial Institutions Examination Council (FFIEC) State Liaison Committee, *Policy Statement on Prudent Commercial Real Estate Loan Workouts* (Oct. 30, 2009) (see for example, Federal Reserve SR 09–07 and FDIC FIL-61-2009); and FDIC, Federal Reserve, OCC, OTS, NCUA, and the Conference of State Bank Regulators, *Interagency Statement on Meeting the Credit Needs of Creditworthy Small Business Borrowers* (Feb. 12, 2010).

[4] Bank examiners review how banks internally classify their loans and assign their own classification to a sample of loans reviewed during an examination. The categories for classification are substandard, doubtful, and loss. Having higher amounts of classified loans can lead to required increases in reserves for future losses on such loans. For more details, see the background section of this report.

[5] All banks that FDIC insures submit quarterly Call Reports, which contain a variety of financial information about a bank's condition and income.

[6] FDIC, the Federal Reserve, and OCC supervise community banks that hold the greatest amount of CRE loans. We did not include OTS or NCUA in our analysis because their institutions hold a relatively small amount of total loans in CRE loans.

[7] FFIEC was established on March 10, 1979, to prescribe uniform principles, standards, and report forms for the federal examination of financial institutions by FDIC, the Federal Reserve, OCC, NCUA, and OTS.

[8] For this analysis, we considered a loan past due after 90 days. Nonaccrual treatment of a loan indicates that the loan is not likely to recover full principal and interest, and therefore the bank cannot recognize the interest it may receive on the loan as income. According to FFIEC call report instructions, generally an asset is to be reported as being in nonaccrual

status if: (1) it is maintained on a cash basis because of deterioration in the financial condition of the borrower, (2) payment in full of principal or interest is not expected, or (3) principal or interest has been in default for a period of 90 days or more unless the asset is both well secured and in the process of collection.

[9] *Concentrations in Commercial Real Estate Lending, Sound Risk Management Practices* sets thresholds for CRE and ADC concentrations, and requires banks to have certain risk-management systems in place to address high concentrations. ADC is considered a risky form of CRE, as it includes loans for constructing and developing commercial real estate projects. We discuss the types of CRE loans and their risks in greater detail in the background section of this report.

[10] See appendix I for additional details on our scope and methodology.

[11] See GAO, *Financial Regulation: A Framework for Crafting and Assessing Proposals to Modernize the Outdated U.S. Financial Regulatory System*, GAO-09-216 (Washington, D.C.: Jan. 8, 2009).

[12] Total capital consists of the sum of tier 1 and tier 2 capital. Tier 1 capital consists primarily of tangible equity. Tier 2 capital includes subordinated debt, a portion of loan loss reserves, and certain other instruments.

[13] These CAMELS definitions are shared among the federal bank regulators; we have excerpted them from the Federal Reserve's *Commercial Bank Examination Manual.*

[14] The regulatory definition of ALLL is the "general valuation allowances that have been established through charges against earnings to absorb losses on loans and lease financing receivables." 12 CFR 325.2.

[15] A charge-off occurs when a bank recognizes that a particular asset or loan will not be collectible and must be written off. This loss is removed from the reserve, or ALLL (which is replenished from income).

[16] These definitions are from *Concentrations in Commercial Real Estate Lending, Sound Risk Management Practices.*

[17] For more information, see E. Philip Davis and Haibin Zhu, "Bank Lending and Commercial Property Cycles: Some Cross-Country Evidence," *Journal for International Money and Finance* 30, no. 1 (2010).

[18] Securitization is a process in which financial assets (such as loans) are brought together into interest-bearing securities that are sold to investors. CMBS are backed by mortgages for CRE, such as apartment and office buildings, industrial properties, hotels, and retail properties. CMBS are sensitive to underlying CRE prices and the cash flow generated from the properties backing the mortgages.

[19] GAO, *Troubled Asset Relief Program: Treasury Needs to Strengthen Its Decision-Making Process on the Term Asset-Backed Securities Loan Facility* (Washington, D.C.: Feb. 5, 2010).

[20] Sam Chandan, Real Capital Analytics, "Commercial Real Estate and Capital Markets Outlook," presentation at FFIEC's Supervisory Updates and Emerging Issues conference in Washington, D.C., on October 20, 2010.

[21] Mortgage Bankers Association, *Commercial Real Estate/Multifamily Finance Quarterly Databook: Third Quarter 2010* (Washington, D.C.: Dec. 21, 2010).

[22] Moody's Investors Service, "U.S. CMBS: Moody's CMBS Delinquency Tracker" (New York: Feb. 14, 2011).

[23] See E. Philip Davis and Haibin Zhu, "Bank Lending and Commercial Property Cycles."

[24] Although there are 106 MLR reports, they address findings on 109 banks.

[25] GAO, *Troubled Asset Relief Program: Status of Programs and Implementation of GAO Recommendations*, GAO-11-74 (Washington, D.C.: January 2011).

[26] Bank for International Settlements, "Cycles and the Financial System," in *71st Annual Report* (2001): 126.

[27] In 2008, the average net portion of the quarterly survey's respondents who said that they were tightening standards for CRE loans was 81.7 percent. This trend of tightening underwriting

standards continued in 2009 and 2010, although at a decreased rate. The average net portion of the quarterly survey's respondents in 2009 who reported tightening standards for CRE loans was 56.4 percent, decreasing to an average of 12.2 percent in 2010.

[28] Concentrations in Commercial Real Estate Lending, Sound Risk Management Practices, Proposed Guidance, 71 Fed. Reg. 2302 (Jan. 13, 2006).

[29] 71 Fed. Reg. 74580 (Dec. 12, 2006). The guidance focuses on CRE loans that are sensitive to conditions in the general CRE market, such as market demand, changes in vacancy rates, and other factors. Based on the approach in the guidance, CRE primarily consists of loans secured by land and development construction, multifamily property, and nonfarm nonresidential property (where the primary source of repayment is derived from rental income associated with the property or the proceeds of the sale, refinancing, or permanent financing of the property). Also included are loans to real estate investment trusts and unsecured loans to developers. Excluded from this definition are loans secured by nonfarm nonresidential properties where the primary source of repayment is the cash flow from the ongoing operations and activities conducted by the party that owns the property.

[30] 71 Fed. Reg. at 74584, 74587.

[31] *Policy Statement on Prudent Commercial Real Estate Loan Workouts* (Oct. 30, 2009).

[32] The 2009 CRE loan workout guidance states the following about identifying a TDR: "a restructured loan is considered a TDR when the institution, for economic or legal reasons related to a borrower's financial difficulties, grants a concession to the borrower in modifying or renewing a loan that the institution would not otherwise consider. To make this determination, the lender assesses whether (a) the borrower is experiencing financial difficulties, and (b) the lender has granted a concession."

[33] GAO, *Standards for Internal Control in the Federal Government*, GAO/AIMD-00.21.3.1 (Washington, D.C.: November 1999).

[34] FFIEC, working with FDIC officials, also introduced a course on CRE loan workouts to supplement existing courses on CRE for commissioned examiners across the banking regulators. Examiners typically are commissioned after they complete professional training and pass tests to measure their proficiency. FFIEC courses are geared toward commissioned examiners from the federal banking regulators and some state regulators.

[35] For example, FDIC headquarters conducts periodic reviews of its regions. The reviews can focus on issues such as the region's timeliness, effectiveness, risk assessment, communication, and systems and also may focus on particular risk areas identified in a region. At the Federal Reserve, the Federal Reserve Board and Reserve Banks conduct a number of internal reviews. First, the Federal Reserve Board reviews certain operations of the Reserve Banks, including risk-focused reviews of each supervision department about every 3 years. Second, each Reserve Bank has a General Auditor who conducts audits of the Supervision and Regulation function about every 3 years. The audits tend to focus on processes and controls. Third, the Reserve Banks have a Quality Assurance function that conducts periodic reviews on whether Supervision and Regulation is executing its responsibilities according to Federal Reserve Board policy guidance.

[36] Of FDIC's six regions, we reviewed the most recent FDIC internal review reports for four (Atlanta, Dallas, New York, and San Francisco).

[37] The Federal Reserve districts that conducted this review are Atlanta, Kansas City, Philadelphia, and Richmond.

[38] This official clarified that the sample of loans was small because he only reviewed downgraded CRE loans, and the volume of downgraded loans in recent ROEs was small.

[39] As part of this process, the districts categorized banks based on their CRE-related risks and reviewed CRE loan classifications for banks that presented the greatest risks. In some cases, this process resulted in changes to loan classifications before the ROE was finalized. We reviewed the reports that all of OCC's districts produced from their quality assurance processes.

[40] OCC could not provide comparable quantitative results for the southern or northeastern districts.

[41] Each survey is used for different purposes. For example, FDIC issues a survey after safety and soundness examinations to seek input from banks to improve the efficiency and effectiveness of the examination process. Other surveys are issued to respond to specific information needs, as discussed above.

[42] The ombudsman offices provide confidentiality, as required by law, and must follow up on any concerns that banks have about potential retaliation from the issues that they have raised with the ombudsman, as detailed in the Riegle Community Development and Regulatory Improvement Act of 1994, Pub. L. No. 103-325 § 309(d), 12 U.S.C. § 4806(d).

[43] Throughout the report, we avoid providing specific numbers of bank officials making certain statements to avoid overstating the precision of the results from the nonprobability sample we selected. For information on how we use the terms "a few," "some," and "many," see appendix I.

[44] In addition, FDIC in March 2011 sent out a reminder to banks about the ways they can contact regulatory officials, and encouraged them to discuss examination concerns. FDIC Financial Institution Letter FL-13-2011, March 1, 2011.

[45] For more details on how we identified these banks for interviews, see appendix I. Because we selected a nonprobability sample, these banks' views are not representative of all banks in the country.

[46] The amount of allowance that a bank provisions in anticipation of potential losses is determined by calculations performed under two accounting standards, Accounting Standards Codification (ASC) 450, Contingencies (formerly FAS 5) and ASC 310-40 (formerly FAS 114). Under ASC 450, segments of the loan portfolio are evaluated on the basis of risk factors such as historical losses, delinquencies and nonaccruals, and concentrations of credit, among other factors. A determination on expected loss rates is made for each loan segment based on the relevant risk factors. Under ASC 310-40, a bank must identify for individual review loans that have been determined to be impaired. The bank should provision for the difference between the book value and the determined market value. The sum of the ASC 450 and 310-40 calculations is the total ALLL.

[47] For additional details on how loan classifications and increased provisions for loan losses affect ALLL, see appendix II.

[48] Specifically, bankers told us that some examiners were using tier 1 capital plus ALLL as the denominator for calculating the concentration, rather than total capital as described in the guidance.

[49] The IGs for FDIC, the Federal Reserve, and Treasury (for OCC and OTS) are required to perform an MLR to determine the cause of bank failures that result in a material loss to the Deposit Insurance Fund and assess the quality of regulatory supervision preceding the failure. See 12 U.S.C. § 1831o(k). Before the Dodd-Frank Wall Street Reform and Consumer Protection Act of 2010, the IGs were required to conduct these reviews when the Deposit Insurance Fund experienced a loss exceeding the greater of $25 million or 2 percent of the bank's assets at the time of FDIC assistance. In the act, Congress amended the provision by increasing the MLR threshold so that it is based on estimated losses exceeding specified amounts. Under the act, IGs are required to conduct MLRs when losses to the Deposit Insurance Fund exceed $200 million during the period from January 1, 2010, to December 31, 2011. This threshold decreases over time to $50 million on or after January 2014. The act also requires the IGs to review all other losses incurred by the Deposit Insurance Fund to determine (a) the grounds identified by the bank's regulator for appointing FDIC as receiver and (b) whether any unusual circumstances exist that might warrant an in-depth review of the loss. Pub. L. No. 111-203 § 987.

[50] For additional details, see GAO, *Financial Regulation: Review of Regulators' Oversight of Risk-management Systems at a Limited Number of Large, Complex Financial Institutions,* GAO-09-499T (Washington, D.C.: Mar. 18, 2009).

[51] The findings of the Financial Crisis Inquiry Commission mirror some MLR findings in stating that leading up to the financial crisis, regulators had tools at their disposal to address growing risks in the financial system but did not always choose to use them. For example, regulators' bank ratings continued to reflect that they were safe and sound, and regulators downgraded ratings only immediately before the banks failed. The report also includes testimony from the Federal Reserve's former director of Banking Supervision and Regulation that prior to the financial crisis, regulatory intervention before a bank showed poor financial performance could have been considered "overly intrusive" or "heavy-handed." See Financial Crisis Inquiry Commission, *The Financial Crisis Inquiry Report: Final Report of the National Commission on the Causes of the Financial and Economic Crisis in the United States* (Washington, D.C.: January 2011).

[52] For more information on our nonprobability sampling of banks for interviews and ROE analysis, see appendix I.

[53] Of the 7 ROEs, 1 was conducted by the Federal Reserve (of 12 Federal Reserve examinations we reviewed); 3 by OCC (of 22 OCC examinations), and 3 by FDIC (of 21 FDIC examinations). Two were for banks in California, one in Georgia, and four in Texas. Note that the sample we selected cannot be extrapolated to the universe of examinations and, therefore, cannot be used to draw conclusions about potential differences among regulators or among banks in certain states.

[54] In two other ROEs, the examination states that the bank must reduce CRE concentrations and the enforcement action also requires at least consideration that concentrations be reduced—although the enforcement action also emphasizes the need for improvements to the bank's risk-management systems.

[55] Specifically, 10 ROEs use only tier 1 capital or tier 1 capital plus ALLL. Another 13 use tier 1 and also provide concentrations as a percent of "capital," but the ROEs are unclear on the form of capital. Thirteen ROEs use total risk-based capital, equity capital, or capital alone. Eleven ROEs use total risk-based capital with tier 1 capital plus ALLL. Eight ROEs either do not provide a concentration or do not clearly articulate how it was calculated.

[56] For more details on whom we interviewed, see appendix I. The views of this particular group of examiners and officials cannot be generalized to the population of all examiners or officials.

[57] For additional details on the potential impact of capital and ALLL on a bank's ability to lend, see appendix II.

[58] Joe Peek and Eric S. Rosengren, "Bank Regulatory Agreements in New England," *New England Economic Review* (May/June 1995): 1-2.

[59] Joe Peek and Eric S. Rosengren, "The Capital Crunch in New England," *New England Economic Review* (May/June 1992): 9.

[60] During the crisis, the average estimated growth rate of non-CRE loans at low- and mid-CRE banks was "positive and around 1 percent." However, during the crisis banks with high CRE concentrations decreased non-CRE lending "on average, by 0.5 percentage points per quarter." These changes led to a "nearly $82 billion cumulative increase in non-CRE loans at low- and mid-CRE banks…and about a $15 billion decline in non-CRE loans at high-CRE banks." "Low-CRE banks and mid-CRE banks" are based on the ratio of CRE loans to total assets right before the onset of the crisis (second quarter of 2007). The bank holding companies were categorized into three groups: high-CRE banks (top 30 percent), mid-CRE banks (30 to 69 percent), and low-CRE banks (bottom 30 percent). Sumit Agarwal, Hesna Genay, and Robert McMenamin (Federal Reserve Bank of Chicago), "Why Aren't Banks Lending More? The Role of Commercial Real Estate," *Chicago Fed Letter* 281 (2010): 1-4. This paper measures changes in loan growth based on changes in total loan assets measured in bank call reports. As we previously have reported, this approach is limited because reductions in total loan balances can be explained by charge-offs and loan payoffs and do not therefore provide an ideal measure of new loan originations. For more information, see GAO, *Troubled Asset Relief Program: Treasury's Framework for Deciding to Extend TARP*

Was Sufficient, but Could Be Strengthened for Future Decisions, GAO-10-531 (Washington, D.C.: June 30, 2010).

[61] In this article, supervisory "toughness" refers to "treating banks of a given financial condition more harshly than in previous years." Allen N. Berger, Margaret K. Kyle, and Joseph M. Scalise, "Did U.S. Bank Supervisors Get Tougher during the Credit Crunch? Did They Get Easier during the Banking Boom? Did It Matter to Bank Lending?" *National Bureau of Economic Research Working Paper Series* 7689 (Cambridge, Mass.: 2000): 1.

[62] We use "CAMEL" in this instance, because that is the term the authors used in the article. See Berger, Kyle, and Scalise, "Did U.S. Bank Supervisors Get Tougher during the Credit Crunch?"

[63] We use "CAMEL" in these instances, because that is the term the authors used in the article. Timothy J. Curry, Gary S. Fissel, and Carlos D. Ramirez, "The Impact of Bank Supervision on Loan Growth," *North American Journal of Economics and Finance* 19 (2008): 113-134.

[64] The tables on pp. 125-130 report aggregate loan growth regressions for three loan categories: commercial and industrial loans (C & I), consumer loans, and real estate loans over two distinct periods: 1985–1993 (first period) and 1994–2004 (second period). Explanatory variables included: (a) first and second lagged dependent variables (loan growth); (b) changes in CAMEL rating (first and second lags); (c) changes in SCOR rating (first and second lag); (d) state output growth (first and second lags). As a group, the tables show a consistent set of results; in all tables (composite CAMEL ratings and components) downgrades are associated with a decline in C&I lending in the first period, but not in the second. In virtually all regressions, the estimated coefficient ranges from about -0.4 to about -0.8 in the short run and the long run. The same is not true, for the most part, for consumer lending or real estate lending. Curry, Fissel, and Ramirez, "The Impact of Bank Supervision on Loan Growth."

[65] A recent memorandum attached to a report from FDIC's IG suggests this when stating that one of FDIC's primary challenges will be to continue its Forward Looking Supervision program even into the next economic recovery period. For the report itself, see FDIC, Office of Inspector General, *Follow-up Audit of FDIC Supervision Program Enhancements,* MLR-11-010 (Arlington, Va.: Dec. 23, 2010).

[66] Discussions on capital requirements among banks and regulators recognize that capital requirements can impact lending—although there is disagreement on the magnitude of that impact. For example, according to an analysis by the Bank for International Settlements, a 4 percentage point increase in the risk-based capital ratio would increase loan interest rates by 60 basis points. In contrast, the Institute for International Finance estimates that a 4 percentage point increase in the risk-based capital ratio would increase loan interest rates by 136 basis points. Therefore, it appears that capital requirements can affect lending, but the severity of such impacts is not completely settled. See Basel Committee on Banking Supervision, *An Assessment of the Long-term Economic Impact of Stronger Capital and Liquidity Requirements* (Basel, Switzerland: August 2010) and two reports from the Institute of International Finance*: Interim Report on the Cumulative Impact on the Global Economy of Proposed Changes in the Banking Regulatory Framework* (Washington, D.C.: June 2010) and *The Net Cumulative Economic Impact of Banking Sector Regulation: Some New Perspectives* (Washington, D.C.: October 2010).

[67] FASB, "Accounting for Financial Instruments and Revisions to the Accounting for Derivative Instruments and Hedging Activities," proposed accounting standards update issued on May 26, 2010.

[68] FDIC, the Federal Reserve, and OCC supervise community banks that hold the most amount of CRE loans. We did not include Office of Thrift Supervision or National Credit Union Administration in our analysis because their institutions hold a relatively small amount of their total loans in CRE loans.

[69] CAMELS encompass Capital adequacy, Asset quality, Management, Earnings, Liquidity, and Sensitivity to market risk. As discussed earlier in this report, in examinations a bank is rated

for each of the CAMELS components and given a composite rating, which generally bears a close relationship to the component ratings. However, the composite is not an average of the component ratings. The component rating and the composite ratings are scored on a scale of 1 (best) to 5 (worst).

[70] For this analysis, we considered a loan past due after 90 days. Nonaccrual treatment of a loan indicates that the loan is not likely to recover full principal and interest, and therefore the bank cannot recognize the interest it may receive on the loan as income. According to call report instructions from the Federal Financial Institutions Examination Council (FFIEC), generally an asset is to be reported as being in nonaccrual status if: (1) it is maintained on a cash basis because of deterioration in the financial condition of the borrower, (2) payment in full of principal or interest is not expected, or (3) principal or interest has been in default for a period of 90 days or more unless the asset is both well secured and in the process of collection.

[71] One ROE in our sample was completed before the guidance was issued in its final form, but it refers to the 2009 guidance, and therefore we included it because it was relevant to our work.

[72] This example is simplified to clarify the relationships between assets and capital.

INDEX

D

E

S

T

U

V

W

Y